MEDIA LAW IN TENNESSEE

MEDIA LAW IN TENNESSEE

By Dorothy A. Bowles

NEW FORUMS PRESS INC.
Stillwater, Oklahoma U.S.A.

This book may be ordered in bulk quantities at discount from New Forums Press, Inc., P.O. Box 876, Stillwater, OK 74076 [Federal I.D. No. 73-1123239].
Printed in the United States of America.

International Standard Book Number: 0-913507-43-1

Table of Contents

About the Author

Dorothy A. Bowles is a faculty member in the School of Journalism at the University of Tennessee, Knoxville. She has worked as a reporter, sports editor, copy editor, and news editor at newspapers in Louisiana, Texas, Wisconsin and Kansas. Her previously published books include *Kansas Media Law Guide* and textbooks in editing and reporting. Articles and reviews she authored have appeared in *Journalism Quarterly, Newspaper Research Journal, Communications and the Law, American Journalism, Journalism History, Media Law Notes, Scholastic Editor, Grassroots Editor* and the *Dictionary of Literary Biography*. She received a Ph.D. with an emphasis in communications law from the University of Wisconsin.

Preface

This book contains a general overview of mass communications law and a comprehensive review of Tennessee statutes and court decisions concerning the legal rights of the mass media. The intended audiences for Media Law in Tennessee are journalists, both print and broadcast, and students interested in journalism, broadcasting, advertising or law. Attorneys representing media clients will also find the book helpful.

The book begins with a discussion of the legal system in Tennessee, including the sources of law, an outline of the state and federal court systems and the penalties for criminal convictions in the state. The second section deals with access to government records and meetings, courtrooms and public and private places where newsworthy events occur. The next part of the book discusses government interference with the news gathering process. Section Four deals with legal restrictions on media content, including the law concerning defamation, privacy, advertising and obscenity. The final chapter in the book offers journalists some tips on avoiding legal problems.

An effort has been made not to overwhelm readers with statute and case citations in the body of the text, but legal references are carefully documented at the end of each chapter to make the book more useful for attorneys and others wishing to consult primary materials. Those who use this book are cautioned that the law of mass communications is a constantly changing field. To address those changes, the publisher plans to issue annual updates. In addition, readers are reminded that for legal questions it is often dangerous to generalize from one fact situation to another.

Special thanks goes to Rebekah V. Bromley, assistant professor at Virginia Tech, who conducted the research for and wrote the chapters on the state and federal court systems and access to the judiciary. Appreciation is expressed to the Bickel Foundation for partially funding Dr. Bromley's final year of doctoral studies at the University of Tennessee and to the UT College of Communications for allowing her time to do research for those chapters as part of her graduate assistantship.

I wish to express appreciation also to Steve Thorpe and Jean Moore, reference librarians at the UT School of Law. Mr. Thorpe was especially helpful in arranging for the author to gain computer access to legal materials.

This book is dedicated to my mother, Gladys Huddleston.

Dorothy A. Bowles
June 1993

MEDIA LAW IN TENNESSEE

"Update" Supplement Request Form

To alert the publisher that you desire to be notifed when each "Update" Supplement for *Media Law in Tennessee* is published, simply fill in your name and permanent mailing address below and send this form to the publisher. Your name and address will be placed on file and you will receive an order form by mail when each yearly supplement is ready—outlining how much it will cost and providing a description of the additions and/or changes it contains.

Send "Update" Supplement order forms to:

Name

Address

City/State/Zip Code

Send this form to: Service Dept., New Forums Press, P.O. Box 876, Stillwater, OK 74076.

Sources of Law in Tennessee

Before considering specific aspects of Tennessee law affecting the mass media, journalists need to understand that answers to their legal questions may come from several sources: constitutional law, statutory law, common law, administrative law or perhaps from an action in equity.

Constitutional Law

The supreme law of the land is the United States Constitution. Any act of the U. S. Congress, state constitutional provision, legislative or administrative action that conflicts with the federal constitution is invalid. The most important part of the U. S. Constitution for journalists is the First Amendment, which reads as follows:

> Congress shall make no law respecting an establishment of religion, or prohibiting the free exercise thereof; or abridging the freedom of speech, or of the press, or the right of the people peaceably to assemble, and to petition the Government for a redress of grievances.

Note that this prohibition applies to Congress, not the states. When the First Amendment and other nine amendments comprising the Bill of Rights were written, they were meant to allay fears that the federal government would impinge on states' rights or deny basic liberties to citizens.[1] Indeed, state legislatures enacted laws that we would recognize today as unconstitutional infringements on free expression. Examples included statutes forbidding the publication or distribution of abolitionist literature and seditious libel laws.

In 1925[2] the U. S. Supreme Court interpreted the due process clause of the Fourteenth Amendment[3] as preventing states from abridging freedom of expression. The due process clause provides as follows:

> No State shall make or enforce any law which shall abridge the privileges or immunities of citizens of the United States; nor shall any State deprive any person of life, liberty, or property, without due process of law; nor deny to any person within its jurisdiction the equal protection of the laws.

In incorporating the guarantees of the First Amendment into the due process clause of the Fourteenth Amendment, the Supreme Court reasoned that free expression is a fundamental liberty that states are forbidden to abridge.

Article I of the constitution of the State of Tennessee is a declaration of rights and includes a provision protecting freedom of speech and press. Section 19 provides:

> That the printing presses shall be free to every person to examine the proceedings of the Legislature; or of any branch or officer of the government, and no law shall ever be made to restrain the right thereof. The free communication of thoughts and opinions, is one of the invaluable rights of man, and every citizen may freely speak, write, and print on any subject, being responsible for the abuse of that liberty. But in prosecutions for the publication of papers investigating the official conduct of officers, or men in public capacity, the truth thereof may be given in evidence; and in all indictments for libel, the jury shall have a right to determine the law and the facts, under the direction of the court, as in other criminal cases.

What do these key parts of the federal and state constitutions mean? Under our system of government with its three branches creating a separation of powers and a means of checks and balances, the courts are charged with interpreting constitutional provisions. Many of the court cases discussed in this book deal with judicial interpretations of the U. S. and Tennessee constitutions.

The structure of the federal and Tennessee court system is outlined in the next chapter.

Common Law

Another source of law in the United States is common law, sometimes referred to as "judge-made" or "discovered" law. The entire body of common law that had developed in England during several centuries was transported to the United States, where over time it has been changed and expanded by court decisions. Called common law to distinguish it from ecclesiastical law, this body of law is based on the principle of *stare decisis* – let the decision stand – whereby legal principles established by a judge in one case become the legal precedent for future cases.

This does not mean, however, that common law is static. Quite the contrary, judges are not bound by the principle of *stare decisis.* Common law is flexible to meet the demands of changing times because judges have the authority to *distinguish* a present case, meaning that the judge can decide that the factual situation differs somewhat from previous cases and thus demands a different outcome.

In addition, if the factual situation in a case is virtually identical to that of a previous case, judges still are not bound by precedent. They may determine that in light of modern-day conditions, an unfair or unworkable decision would result from following precedent. Thus, judges may decide to *overturn or reverse* precedent.

Common law deals with real cases and controversies, meaning that courts do not give advisory opinions. They must be presented with specific factual situations involving specific people who have been accused of a crime or who claim injury.

Legal principles that have developed through common law are not available in a single place. Rather, courts publish their decisions in volumes called "case reporters," with cases arranged chronologically according to the date of the decision. Each level of courts has at least one case reporter.

The current case reporter for U. S. District Courts is titled *Federal Supplement,* abbreviated in citations as *F. Supp.* Many district court decisions are "unreported," meaning that they do not appear in the *Federal Supplement.* Decisions that deal with procedural rules for the district courts appear in *Federal Rules Decisions* (F.R.D.) instead of the *Federal Supplement.*

Federal courts of appeal decisions are reported in the *Federal Reporter,* Second Series, cited as F.2d.

U. S. Supreme Court decisions can be found in several different reporters. The official reporter, published by the government, is *U. S. Reports,* cited as *U.S.* In addition, privately owned publishing companies produce books containing case opinions from the highest court. These are the *Supreme Court Reporter* (S.Ct.) and the *U. S. Supreme Court Reports, Lawyers' Edition, Second Series,* abbreviated *L.Ed.2d.*

Tennessee Supreme Court decisions are recorded in the *Tennessee Reports,* abbreviated Tenn., and the title of the reporter for decisions of the state court of appeals is *Tennessee Appeals* (Tenn. App.). *The Tennessee Criminal Appeals Reports* (Tenn. Crim. App.) includes decisions of the Court of Criminal Appeals.

To decrease the cost of buying sets of reporters from all each states, many law firms and libraries subscribe to *regional reporters* published by West Publishing Company. These reporters include many, but not all, of the opinions issued by state courts. Tennessee opinions are included in the *South Western Reporter,* now in its second series and abbreviated S.W.2d.

Another source of court opinions that you will see cited in the chapter end notes in this book is *Media Law Reporter.* This is a compilation of selected state and federal court decisions pertaining to communications law.

The form for court citations is the volume number, followed by the abbreviation for the appropriate reporter, followed by the page number on which the opinion begins. For example, the citation for *New York Times v. Sullivan,* an important libel case, is "376 U.S. 254" meaning that this particular case is in Volume 376 of the *U. S. Reports*, beginning on page 254.

Statutory Law

Another source of law is statutory law, that made by legislative bodies, including the U. S. Congress and the Tennessee General Assembly. State entities such as cities and counties also enact laws referred to as "ordinances."

Statutory law generally concerns society as a whole rather than the problems of an individual. Too, statutory law, unlike common law, can anticipate societal problems rather than waiting for a real case and controversy to arise. Legislative bodies, for example, can enact laws concerning proper driving without waiting for someone to sue for damages after an automobile injury.

When bills are passed into law, they are assigned a number. For example, P.L. 100-30 means that this was the 30th public law passed by the 100th session of Congress. After the session ends, all laws are published in code books.

A person wishing to find a particular federal statute can use the *United States Statutes at Large,* abbreviated Stat., to find laws printed in the chronological order of enactment, or the *United States Code* (U.S.C.) where the statutes are arranged according to subject matter. The citation for the Communications Act of 1934, for example, is 48 Stat. 1064, meaning that this law can be found in Volume 48 of the *United States Statutes at Large* on page 1064. The same statute may be cited as 47 U.S.C. 151 et seq., which means Title 47 of the *U. S. Code* section 151 and following.

Statutes passed by each session the Tennessee General Assembly are compiled chronologically in volumes titled *Public Acts of the State of Tennessee* (Tenn. Pub. Acts). The statutes are also compiled according to subject matter in the *Tennessee Code Annotated* (Tenn. Code Ann.)

Administrative Law

The rules and regulations passed by federal and state administrative agencies are another source of law. To deal with an ever increasingly complex society, Congress and state legislatures have created agencies, boards and commissions and given them power to enact rules and regulations with the force of law within specified areas of expertise. These administrative bodies must work within the authority that Congress or the Tennessee General Assembly granted them in their enabling legislation.

As a check on that power, their work of administrative agencies is subject to court review. Further, what Congress gives, Congress can take away, meaning that Congress, or a state legislature in the case of a state agency, may retract power it has granted and may also exercise control of the agencies through the power of the purse.

Although Congress created the federal agencies, they are considered a part of the executive branch with members appointed by the president and subject to Senate confirmation. Two federal agencies of special importance to media organizations are the Federal Communications Commission and the Federal Trade Commission.

Like statutes, administrative rules are compiled both chronologically and according to subject matter. *The Federal Register* (Fed. Reg.) includes a chronological collection, and the rules are arranged by subject matter in the *Code of Federal Regulations* (C.F.R.).

In addition, many of the federal agencies issue publications. For example, the rules and regulations of the FCC are published in the *Federal Communications Commission Reports,* abbreviated in citations as F.C.C.

Agencies in Tennessee publish a record of their work each month in the *Tennessee Administrative Register* (Tenn. Admin. Reg.), and the subject area compilation is called the *Official Compilation Rules & Regulations of the State of Tennessee,* abbreviated Tenn. Comp. R. & Regs.

Equity Action

Equity is an alternative to law that may be used where no adequate legal remedy is available. As noted earlier in this chapter, common law deals with real cases and controversies; the courts won't become involved in the matter until the damage has been done.

A party seeking to head off potential damage might ask a court to grant equitable relief. A judge would determine what would be fair in the particular situation and might decide to grant relief in the form of an injunction ordering that a particular action cease. An example of equity in communications law is an injunction ordering a news organization not to publish information that would endanger national security.

The matter would not necessarily end with the granting of the injunction, however, because the news organization could go to court to challenge its constitutional validity. Courts do not allow prior restraints on publication except in highly unusual circumstances; therefore, the party seeking the injunction – the federal government in this example – would have the burden of proving that publication would cause direct, immediate and irreparable harm.[4] If the government is unable to meet this burden of proof, the court will lift the injunction, meaning that the news organization would be free to publish the material.

Endnotes

1. The First Amendment was ratified by the states on Dec. 15, 1791.

2. Gitlow v. New York, 268 U.S. 652.

3. The Fourteenth Amendment was ratified July 9, 1868.

4. See, for example, the "Pentagon Papers" case: New York Times v. U.S., 403 U.S. 713 (1971).

The Court System in Tennessee

State Courts

The Tennessee Constitution provides that the judicial power of Tennessee resides with the supreme court and in other inferior courts as created by the legislature.[1] The state court system consists of three tiers of courts (See Table 1). Occupying the top tier is the supreme court, which has supervisory authority over all Tennessee courts. The second tier comprises the intermediate appellate courts: the court of criminal appeals and the court of appeals. The third tier of the state court system consists of the trial courts: the criminal courts, circuit courts and chancery courts.

In addition to the state courts, specialized courts on the local level can be said to occupy a fourth tier of courts in Tennessee. These courts include general sessions, juvenile, municipal and probate courts. Two counties, Anderson and Sevier, have trial justice courts, which are similar to general sessions courts but with broader jurisdiction.[2] Viewed as courts of limited jurisdiction, the local courts have authority over local ordinances plus limited jurisdiction concerning matters such as traffic violations, misdemeanors, small claims and juveniles.

The court system in Tennessee is complex and somewhat confusing because of its lack of consolidation. For example, Tennessee has two levels of trial courts: one in the state system and another at the local level. And, Tennessee is one of few states with both chancery and circuit courts. At the state level, the jurisdiction of the courts may also be concurrent. Additionally, the jurisdiction of local courts may overlap within a municipality, and jurisdiction may vary from municipality to municipality.

Supreme Court

The supreme court meets three times each year in Knoxville and Nashville and twice each year in Jackson. The court may not be altered or abolished by the General Assembly.[3]

TABLE 1
Tennessee Court System

State Courts			
Supreme Court			
Court of Appeals		Court of Criminal Appeals	
Criminal Courts	Circuit Courts		Chancery Courts
Local Courts			
General Sessions Courts	Juvenile Courts	Municipal Courts	Probate Courts

From the Tennessee Judicial Council Annual Report 1989-1990, p. 7

Chief Justice

The chief justice of the supreme court is designated by the court's justices for a 19-month term. The position is rotated among the members. As administrative head of the state court system, the chief justice may appoint judges to serve in the state court system if a vacancy occurs before election.. The chief justice also presides at the trial of any public official who may be impeached under the state constitution, certifies to the governor the disability of a judge and is chairman of the Law Library Commission, Tennessee Code Commission and the commission that oversees the supreme court buildings in Knoxville, Nashville and Jackson.

Jurisdiction

The supreme court does not have original jurisdiction in any matter (See Table 2). The court's jurisdiction is appellate; however, direct appeals may be made to the supreme court in questions concerning the constitutionality of a state law or municipal ordinance, conviction in a death penalty case, and cases concerning the right to hold public office and worker's compensation.

Typically, appeals are made to the supreme court from an intermediate court by an application for permission to appeal, but appeals may come to the court on direct appeal from a simple appeal, a writ of error or a appeal in error. In the simple appeal, which originates in cases heard in chancery court, the supreme court may review questions of both fact and law and may give a new judgement. The court may only remand and return a case for a new trial if the appeal comes in the form of a writ of error or as an appeal in error. For example, in appeals made in the form of a writ of error, the court reviews the trial record only to determine whether there has been an error of law. Except for death penalty cases, the court's decision to accept a case on appeal is discretionary.

Decisions by the Tennessee supreme court are subject to review by the Supreme Court of the United States.[4]

Intermediate Courts of Appeals

Court of Appeals

The court of appeals was established by the legislature to hear civil cases. Appeals reach the court in two ways: by right or by permission from inferior courts. The court of appeals hears civil appeals from the state trial courts that do not directly go to the supreme court. In cases concerning constitutional questions, the court's jurisdiction extends only to the transfer of the appeals to the supreme court.[5]

Court of Criminal Appeals

The court of appeals was established by the legislature and, therefore, may be altered or even abolished by the legislature.

The criminal appeals court hears criminal cases from inferior courts that do not go directly to the supreme court. For example, appeals of death penalty convictions may be made directly to the supreme court.

State Trial Courts

Each of the state's 31 judicial districts has a circuit court, but chancery and criminal trial courts do not operate within every judicial district. There are 25 chancery courts established in the 31 judicial districts and 13 criminal courts (See Table 3). The Tennessee Blue Book for 1989-1990 reported 33 chancellors for the chancery courts, 69 judges for the circuit courts and 26 justices serving as criminal court judges.

Tennessee is one of few states with separate circuit and chancery courts. Chancery courts generally hear cases of equity. In areas that do not have chancellors, chancery cases are heard by circuit judges. In areas without criminal courts, the circuit courts have jurisdiction. Jurisdiction of the courts may be altered at the discretion of the legislature.[6]

TABLE 2
State Appellate Courts

	Supreme Court	Court of Appeals	Court of Criminal Appeals
		Judges	
Number	5	12	9
Selection	Statewide General Election	Governor selects 1 of 3 nominees of commission for first term, then judges run unopposed in general election on retention or rejection basis. Nominees are selected from the grand division with a vacancy.	
Term	Eight years	Eight years	Eight years
Qualifications	Min. age 35, resident of state five years, licensed to practice law in state, U.S. citizen	Minimum age of 30, resident of state for five years, licensed to practice law in state.	
(Continued on next page.)			

TABLE 2 (continued).

Limitations	No more than two justices may reside in same grand division.	No more than four justices in the appeals court or three justices in the criminal appeals court may reside in the same grand division.	
		Court	
Jurisdiction	Appellate. Discretionary authority to review all cases from lower courts except must grant application for review in death penalty convictions.	All civil cases, except constitutionality of statutes and ordinances, worker's comp., and right to hold office. May review orders of state agencies, actions of boards and commissions, and paternity cases.	Felony and misdemeanor appeals, post-conviction petitions.
Site(s)	The court may sit where the chief justice designates, but is required to sit in Knoxville (September), in Nashville (December) and Jackson (April).	Justices may sit in 4 sections of 3 judges, two sections of 6 judges or en banc. The court sits in panels concurrently in Knoxville, Nashville and Jackson.	May sit in panels of 3, 5, or 7 justices. Is required to sit in Knoxville (June), Nashville (February) and Jackson (October).

A judge or chancellor in the trial courts is elected to an eight-year term by voters in the circuit or district where the trial court is located. To be eligible for office, a judge must be at least 30 years old and have been a resident of the state for five years and a resident of the district or circuit for one year prior to the election. The state constitution requires that judges in state trial courts, but not local courts, be authorized to practice law in

Tennessee. For state trial courts, the governor makes direct appointments to fill interim vacancies.

In some matters, the trial courts have concurrent jurisdiction. For example, in matters such as divorce and the recovery of property, the circuit and chancery courts have concurrent jurisdiction. Similarly, the circuit, chancery and criminal courts share jurisdiction in cases concerning a public nuisance and disciplinary proceedings against attorneys.

Criminal Courts

Cases involving the commission of a crime are heard in criminal court, as are misdemeanor cases on appeal from local courts. In criminal cases, a jury decides whether the defendant is guilty and determines the sentence, within sentencing guidelines established by the legislature.[7] A defendant may, however, waive the right to a jury trial. In those instances, a criminal court judge will hear the case and impose a sentence if the defendant is found guilty.

Circuit Courts

The jurisdiction of a circuit court may encompass one or more counties (See Table 3). Circuit courts, possessing general original jurisdiction in civil and criminal cases, have jurisdiction to hear cases not specifically given to another court. However, the circuit court has original jurisdiction in actions such as contested wills, errors in deeds transferring land and cases involving eminent domain. Monetary limits are not placed on cases heard in circuit courts. As a result, damage suits resulting from automobile accidents are typically heard in the courts.

The circuit court has appellate jurisdiction of all suits and actions not given to another court from any inferior court.[8] For example, the circuit court hears appellate cases from general sessions and municipal courts.

TABLE 3
State Judicial Districts and Courts by County

1st — Carter, Johnson, Unicoi, Washington All three trial courts.	**11th** — Hamilton. All three trial courts.	**21st** — Hickman, Lewis, Perry, Williamson. Circuit court only.
2nd — Sullivan. All three trial courts.	**12th** — Bledsoe, Franklin, Grundy, Marion, Rhea, Sequatchie. Circuit and chancery courts.	**22nd** — Giles, Lawrence, Maury, Wayne. Circuit court only.
3rd — Greene, Hamblen, Hancock, Hawkins. All three trial courts.	**13th** — Clay, Cumberland, DeKalb, Overton, Pickett, Putnam, White. All three trial courts.	**23rd** — Cheatham, Dickson, Houston, Humphreys, Stewart. Circuit court only.
4th — Cocke, Grainger, Jefferson, Sevier. Circuit and chancery courts.	**14th** — Coffee. Circuit court only.	**24th** — Benton, Carroll, Decatur, Hardin, Henry. Circuit and chancery courts.
5th — Blount. Circuit court only.	**15th** — Jackson, Macon, Smith, Trousdale, Wilson. All three trial courts present.	**25th** — Fayette, Hardeman, Lauderdale, McNairy, Tipton. Circuit and chancery courts.
6th — Knox. All three trial courts.	**16th** — Cannon, Rutherford. Circuit and chancery courts.	**26th** — Chester, Henderson, Madison. Circuit and chancery courts.
7th — Anderson. Circuit and chancery courts.	**17th** — Bedford, Lincoln, Marshall, Moore. Circuit and chancery courts.	**27th** — Obion, Weakley. Circuit and chancery courts.
8th — Campbell, Claiborne, Fentress, Scott, Union. All three trial courts.	**18th** — Sumner. All three trial courts.	**28th** — Crockett, Gibson, Haywood. Circuit and chancery courts.

TABLE 3 (Continued).		
9th — Loudon, Meigs, Morgan, Roane. All three trial courts.	**19th** — Montgomery, Robertson. Circuit and chancery courts.	**29th** — Dyer, Lake. Circuit and chancery courts.
10th — Bradley, McMinn, Monroe, Polk. All three trial courts.	**20th** — Davidson. All three trial courts present.	**30th** — Shelby. All three trial courts.
		31st — Van Buren, Warren. Circuit court only.

Chancery Courts

As with circuit courts, a chancery court's jurisdiction may cover one county or multi-counties. Chancery court jurisdiction extends over all civil matters, concurrent with circuit courts except some damage cases. Chancery courts generally hear cases of equity, a term applied to cases where the existing law does not necessarily provide for a remedy. The judges, or "chancellors" as they are called, apply moral standards of justice to fit the circumstances of a particular case. Civil disputes, matters that do not involve crimes, come before the court when the state, private parties or entities have disagreements with one another.

The chancery court may hear cases about guardianship and the estates of minors.[9] It has jurisdiction, concurrent with the circuit court, for divorce and adoption proceedings.[10] It also has jurisdiction in actions such as disagreements between the state and a corporation and property line disputes. Chancery courts also hear cases on appeal, concurrent with circuit courts, from administrative boards or agencies. Appeal of chancery cases concerning state agency orders or actions of boards and commissions that were established under Tennessee law are made to the court of appeals.

Local Courts

Below the state level, Tennessee has a tier of trial courts, which are funded locally and have limited or special jurisdiction. These include general sessions, probate, juvenile and municipal courts. As a result, a court case in Tennessee originating in the local courts could proceed through four tiers of courts: one local tier and three state tiers. However, a case may skip court tiers or originate at different levels.

General Sessions Courts

General sessions courts have both civil and criminal jurisdiction although the criminal jurisdiction is restricted to misdemeanors when the fine is less than $50 and/or the prison term is less than one year. There are no jury trials in general sessions courts. All but three of Tennessee's 95 counties have a general sessions court. In Anderson and Sevier counties, the trial court is similar to the general sessions courts found in the other counties, except with broader jurisdiction. Stewart County has no lower court.

The jurisdiction of general sessions courts varies according to county in Tennessee. For example, in some counties general sessions courts hear municipal ordinance violations, while other counties have granted the courts authority to hear cases involving probate, domestic relations and juvenile issues. Commonly referred to as small claims courts, general sessions courts' jurisdiction in civil cases is limited to cases with a monetary dispute less than $10,000 in counties with populations less than 700,000 or $15,000 in counties with populations greater than 700,000.

Judges in general sessions courts generally do not have to be attorneys, but are required to be at least 30 years old, a state resident for five years and a county resident for one year.

Probate Courts

Generally hearing cases concerning wills and estates, probate courts do not have appellate jurisdiction or jury trials. For counties without probate courts, cases are heard by the chancery or general sessions courts. Judges are elected for eight-year terms.

Juvenile Courts

Juvenile courts hear cases concerning minors involved in both civil and criminal cases. Although the chancery court has jurisdiction over cases involving minors and the estates of minors, juvenile courts have exclusive jurisdiction in custody cases.[11] Appeals of juvenile court decisions are made to the circuit court.[12] In counties without juvenile courts, the cases are heard by general sessions courts. There are no jury trials in juvenile courts. Judges are elected, and terms of office may vary.

Municipal Courts

The lowest level courts in Tennessee are the municipal courts, which have no uniform subject matter jurisdiction, but primarily handle misdemeanor violations of municipal ordinances or municipal charters. Unless jurisdiction has been specifically granted by the legislature, the courts may not hear cases involving the violation of a state statute. Consequently, without permission of the legislature, cases involving the violation of state vehicle laws may not be brought before municipal traffic courts.[13] Several municipal courts in some matters may have concurrent jurisdiction with general sessions courts. Municipal court fines may not exceed $50 and imprisonment may not exceed 30 days.

The are no jury trials in municipal courts and appeals of the courts' decisions may be heard by either circuit or criminal courts.

The selection and qualification of judges for the municipal courts vary in Tennessee according to locally created procedures. Consequently, judges do not have to be elected, nor are the terms of office necessarily the same for judges serving in different municipalities.[14]

Federal Courts

United States District Courts in Tennessee

U.S. District Courts, trial courts of general federal jurisdiction, hear both civil and criminal cases. Each state has at least one federal district court and some states have as many as four. Within a state, a district court may have more than one division. Tennessee has three district courts, eastern, middle and western.

The eastern district court has four divisions, the middle district has three divisions and the western district has two divisions (See Table 4).

The federal district courts hear the following cases: (a) those arising under the Constitution, laws or treaties of the United States when the amount in controversy exceeds $10,000;[15] (b) actions between citizens of different states or citizens of a state and a foreign government when the amount in controversy exceeds $10,000;[16] if such a case is filed in state courts, it may be removed by one of the parties to the federal court;[17] (c) civil rights cases, election disputes, commerce and antitrust cases, postal matters, Internal Revenue and other enumerated cases.[18]

United States Bankruptcy Courts in Tennessee

In 1984, under the Bankruptcy Code, Congress created a bankruptcy court for each U.S. District. Consequently, there are three bankruptcy courts in Tennessee, one each for the eastern, middle, and western districts. Judges are appointed by the court of appeals judges and serve 14- year terms. Jurisdiction of the courts extends to all civil proceedings under the Bankruptcy Code and cases related to the Code.

United States Courts of Appeals

There are 13 U.S. Courts of Appeals. The numbered courts, 1 through 11, encompass multi-state jurisdictional areas that may be quite large. For example, the 9th Circuit, the largest circuit court of appeals in the nation, hears cases from nine states and two Pacific territories. The two unnumbered intermediate federal appellate courts are the U.S. Court of Appeals for the District of Columbia and the U.S. Federal Court of Appeals. The Federal Court, a nonregional specialized court, has exclusive jurisdiction over such matters as patent validity and infringement. The D.C. Circuit has jurisdictional responsibility for only the District of Columbia.

TABLE 4
Federal District Courts In Tennessee by County

Eastern District	Middle District	Western District
Northeastern Division Carter, Cocke, Greene, Hamblen, Hancock, Hawkins, Johnson, Sullivan, Unicoi, Washington.	*Northeastern Division* Clay, Cumberland, DeKalb, Fentress, Jackson, Macon, Overton, Pickett, Putnam, Smith, White.	*Eastern Division* Benton, Carroll, Chester, Crockett, Decatur, Gibson, Hardeman, Hardin, Haywood, Henderson, Henry, Lake, Madison, McNairy, Obion, Perry, Weakley.
Northern Division Anderson, Blount, Campbell, Claiborne, Grainger, Jefferson, Knox, Loudon, Monroe, Morgan, Roane, Scott, Sevier, Union.	*Nashville Division* Cannon, Cheatham, Davidson, Dickson, Houston, Humphreys, Montgomery, Robertson, Rutherford, Stewart, Sumner, Trousdale, Williamson, Wilson.	*Western Division* Dyer, Fayette, Lauderdale, Shelby, Tipton.
Southern Division Bledsoe, Bradley, Hamilton, Marion, McMinn, Meigs, Polk, Rhea, Sequatchie.	*Columbia Division* Giles, Hickman, Lawrence, Lewis, Marshall, Maury, Wayne	
Winchester Division Bedford, Coffee, Franklin, Grundy, Lincoln, Moore, Van Buren, Warren.		

From *The American Bench,* 1991/1992.

Tennessee is within the jurisdiction of the U.S. Court of Appeals for the Sixth Circuit, along with Kentucky, Ohio and Michigan. The 6th Circuit is based in Cincinnati, Ohio, and typically the court sits in that city. However, the court may sit in any city within the four states in the circuit. The administrative actions and decisions of the 6th Circuit are made public in Cincinnati, and, since January 1, 1990, are available to the public and the media via on-line computer.

The federal appellate courts hear civil and criminal appeals from the state and federal district courts within their geographic jurisdictions. The majority of cases in the appellate courts are private civil actions.[19] The courts of appeals may also hear cases from federal agencies and administrative law judges. The appellate courts answer questions in law, not fact. Because the Supreme Court intervenes infrequently, for most federal litigates "the courts of appeals become the last resort in an overwhelming majority of cases."[20]

As of December 1, 1990, 179 judgeships were authorized for the intermediate federal appellate courts, including 16 for the 6th Circuit.[21] The justices sit in panels of three unless a majority vote to sit en banc. A decision by a panel is binding, as is one by an en banc court. However, a decision within one circuit is not binding on any other circuit. If two circuits disagree, the Supreme Court may settle the issue.

Supreme Court of the United States

At the top of the federal court system is the Supreme Court. The Court has has nine justices, one of whom serves as chief justice. The justices are appointed by the president, subject to the approval of the Senate, and serve for life. It is not uncommon for presidents to select justices based on how presidents think the justices are likely to interpret the Constitution.

During a single term, which runs from October through the following June, the Supreme Court typically is asked to review approximately 5,000 cases. Of these cases the Court chooses to write formal decisions in fewer than 150 each term.

State or federal cases come to the Court in three ways: application for a writ of certiorari, by appeal, and certification. The most common method is certiorari, which justices have discretionary authority to grant or deny. If four of the nine justices agree that a question exists about a federal constitutional principle or point of federal law as applied by a lower court, the Court orders the lower court to forward the records for review.

The Court may choose to accept on direct appeal those cases in which lower courts have decided that state or federal laws violated the Constitution. The Court may also choose not to hear these appeals. Through certification, the courts of appeals may request the Court to clarify a point of law in a pending case. Certification requests are infrequent.

Endnotes

1. Tennessee Constitution, Art. VI, 1.

2. Tennessee Judicial Council Annual Report, 1989-90. Nashville: Office of Executive Secretary to the Tennessee Supreme Court, 1990, p. 159.

3. Tennessee Constitution, Art., VI, § 1.

4. Barger v. Brock, 535 S.W. 2nd 337 (Tenn. 1976).

5. Campbell County v. Wright, 151 S.W. 411 (1912).

6. Bank of State v. Cooper, 10 Tenn. 599 (1831).

7. Criminal Sentencing Reform Act of 1989, T.C.A. 40-35-111.

8. T.C.A. 16-10-112.

9. T.C.A. 16-11-109.

10. T.C.A. 16-11-110.

11. State ex rel. Baker v. Turner, 562 S.W. 2d 435 (Tenn. Ct. App. 1977).

12. State v. Womack, 591 S.W. 2d 437 (Tenn. Ct. App. 1979).

13. Hill v. State ex rel. Phillips, 216 Tenn. 503, 392 S.W. 2d 950 (1960).

14. City of Elizabethton v. Carter County, 204 Tenn. 452, 321 S.W. 2d 822 (1958).

15. 28 U.S.C. §1331.

16. 28 U.S.C. §1332.

17. 28 U.S.C. §1441.

18. 28 U.S.C. §1333-1364.

19. *Annual Report of the Director of the Administrative Office of the United States Courts 1990,* Supplemental Tables, B-1, p. 106.

20. Robert A. Carp and Ronald Stidham, *The Federal Courts* (Washington, D.C.: Congressional Quarterly Press, 1985), p. 36.

21. *The U.S. Government Manual 1991-1992* (Office of the Federal Register, National Archives and Records Administration, 1991), p. 73.

Penalties for Criminal Convictions

The Criminal Sentencing Reform Act of 1989 (T.C.A. 40-35-111) authorized the following terms of imprisonment and fines for felonies and misdemeanors.

Felonies				
CLASS	IMPRISONMENT (YEARS)[a] MINIMUN	MAXIMUM	MAXIMUM FINE[b]	FINE FOR CORP.[c]
A	15	60	$50,000	$350,000
B	8	30	$25,000	$300,000
C	3	15	$10,000	$250,000
D	2	12	$5,000	$125,000
E	1	6	$3,000	$50,000

Misdemeanors		
CLASS	MAXIMUM TERM[d]	MAXIMUM FINE
A	11 months, 29 days	$2,500
B	6 months	$500
C	30 days	$50

[a]Mandatory, determinate sentence.

[b]Fines are not mandatory; jury may determine a fine up to the amount stated here unless otherwise provided by statute.

[c]If a special fine for a corporation is expressly specified in the statute that defines an offense, the fine fixed shall be within the limits specified in the statute.

[d]Punishment for misdemeanor may include a jail term, fine, or both.

Access to Government Records

Openness in government is essential to a democratic society. Citizens can't make informed decisions at the voting booth or in other aspects of their lives without knowing how their elected representatives perform in office. That knowledge comes through observing officeholders at public meetings and through examining the documents and other materials generated by government. But few citizens have the time or inclination to attend meetings or study government records, so they generally depend on the press to serves as their eyes and ears in performing this vital watchdog function on government.

Neither the federal constitution nor the Tennessee constitution has been interpreted as providing a right of access to government information. That right has been granted by the U.S. Congress and the Tennessee General Assembly in the form of statutes that declare records open for public inspection. However, in an effort to balance competing interests – where openness might violate national security or individual privacy, for example – legislators at both the state and federal levels have made certain records confidential and thus exempt from the statutory right of access.

Access in Tennessee

What Records Are Open?

The Tennessee public records law provides that all "state, county and municipal records, as well as all records maintained by the Tennessee performing arts center management corporation, shall at all times, during business hours, be open for personal inspection by any citizen of Tennessee, and those in charge of such records shall not refuse such right of inspection to any citizen, unless otherwise provided by state statutes."[1] The act has been amended several times since the General Assembly originally passed it in 1957.

On its face, the act appears to be a model for openness, but, as described in this chapter, the state legislature has exempted many records that one would probably assume are open for public inspection – like birth, death, marriage and divorce records. Compounding the problem, especially for journalists, is the fact that these exemptions are not spelled out in any one place in the Tennessee statutes. To determine what records have been exempted by state law, one must examine literally hundreds of statutes. These exemptions are discussed in this chapter under the heading "Records Exempt from the State Public Records Act."

Tennessee statutes regarding administrative rules and procedure[2] provide for public inspection and copying of agency rules, final orders and decisions and direct agencies to make available for inspection and copying:

(a) Agency rules, final orders and decisions;
(b) Written statements of policy or interpretations formulated, adopted, or used by the agency in the discharge of its functions;
(c) Opinions of the attorney general rendered to the agency;
(d) A description of its current organization stating the general course and method of its operation and the methods whereby the public may obtain information or make submissions or requests.

Agencies may charge reasonable compensatory fees for providing documents. State statute also provides that if part of a record is closed by state statute, that part may be deleted so that the segregable portion of the document or record can be provided.[3]

Further, whether a record is required by law to be maintained has no bearing on its openness. The fact that material is kept as part of discharging the duties of an office makes it subject to the public records act, unless otherwise made confidential.[4]

What if Access Is Denied?

Any citizen who is denied access to a public record has a right to petition for access and to obtain judicial review of the denial.[5] Citizens should file a petition in the chancery court for the county in which the county or municipal records sought are situated or in any other court of that county having equity jurisdiction. For records in the control of a state agency, a petition for access should be filed in the chancery court of Davidson County or in the chancery court for the county in which the state records are situated if different from Davidson County, or in any other court of that county having equity jurisdiction, or in the chancery court in the county of the petitioner's residence, or in any other court of that county having equity jurisdiction.

Public officials who refuse access must justify the denial by proving by a preponderance of the evidence that the record falls within a statutory exemption.[6]

Petitions for access under the public records act should receive expeditious treatment. The statute specifies that upon filing of the petition, the court shall, upon request of the petitioning party, issue an order requiring the defendant or respondent party to appear immediately and show cause, if any, why the petition should not be granted. The court may direct that the records being sought be submitted under seal for review by the court. The decision of the court on the petition constitutes a final judgment on the merits.[7]

The General Assembly has expressed its intent that courts should broadly interpret the public records act to give the fullest possible public access.[8] In ruling upon petitions for access, courts are instructed to render written findings of fact and conclusions of law and are empowered to exercise full injunctive remedies and relief to secure the purposes and intentions of the act.[9]

If a court rules in favor of access, it should order that the records be made available unless one of the following conditions exists:[10]

- There is a timely filing of a notice of appeal; and
- The court certifies that there exists a substantial legal issue with respect to the disclosure of the documents which ought to be resolved by the appellate courts.

The Tennessee Supreme Court has held that this section does not limit the scope of the public records act nor does it give the courts leeway to exempt records from public inspection.[11]

Liability for Denying Public Records

If a court finds that the custodian of a public record knowingly and willfully denied access, the court may assess all reasonable costs involved in obtaining the record, including attorneys' fees, against the nondisclosing governmental entity.[12] The statute protects public officials from criminal or civil liability for the release of records and relieves officials from being held responsible for damages caused by the release of public information.[13]

Records Exempt from the State Public Records Act

How are exemptions created?

The statute specifies that most exemptions must be created by state statute,[14] but the act gives the head of a governmental entity the authority to promulgate rules in accordance with the Uniform Administrative Procedures Act,[15] to maintain the confidentiality of records concerning adoption proceedings or records required to be kept confidential by federal statute or regulation as a condition for the receipt of federal funds or for participation in a federally funded program.[16]

When it was originally enacted in 1957 the law allowed governmental agencies to create exemptions, but the 1984 General Assembly removed that authority so that the legislature alone now has the authority to create exemptions except for the provision mandating conformity with federal laws or rules, as noted in the previous paragraph. The state supreme court has rejected the argument that state courts should grant exceptions to openness for records on the basis of "public policy," holding that when, as in the case of public records, the legislature takes a position on a particular subject, that position becomes the public policy of the state on that subject.[17]

The General Assembly has given the governor the powered to keep secret information in the office of the secretary of state that relates immediately to the executive department.[18]

What records are exempt?

One section[19] of the public records act lists 10 categories of records as confidential. In addition, cross-references to the act in the Tennessee Code Annotated list more than 80 other exemptions.

Statutes declaring certain records confidential generally provide for access in compliance with a subpoena or court order. In addition, a state court has held that courts, grand juries, and district attorneys are not embraced in the term "public" as used in the "confidential records" section[20] of the public records act,[21] meaning that people serving in these capacities are not denied access to records listed in that statute. In many of the statutes declaring certain records confidential, the legislature included a paragraph providing for legislative inspection by a duly adopted resolution of either house or a standing or joint committee of either house.

The following sections, arranged in alphabetical order, detail records that are exempt by statute from the Tennessee public records act.

Abuse, neglect, or exploitation

Records concerning reports of child sexual abuse, including the name of a person reporting child sexual abuse, reports made to the abuse registry and all records generated as a result of such reports, are confidential.[22]

This information may be released to a law enforcement agency investigating a report of child sexual abuse; the district attorney general of the judicial district in which the child resides or in which the alleged abuse occurred; a grand jury, by subpoena; a court official, probation counselor, parole officer, designated employee of the department of correction or other individual charged with preparing information to be presented in a proceeding concerning a person charged with or convicted of child abuse or neglect.[23] Such information is available to professionals involved with the diagnosis and treatment of the child or the person perpetrating the sexual abuse.[24] The statute also provides that researchers may gain access to general information about child abuse that does not identify specific individuals.[25]

Another statute allows the identity of a person reporting child abuse to be revealed in a juvenile court proceeding if the court, in its discretion, determines that the testimony is material to an indictment or conviction.[26] However the statute mandates that the identity of the reporter is not subject to disclosure by court order in a civil proceeding.[27]

Child sexual abuse autopsy reports are open, as the legislature has exempted them from confidentiality requirements for other child sexual abuse material.[28]

The identity of a person who reports abuse, neglect, or exploitation under the Adult Protection Act is confidential.[29]

Accident reports

Accident reports made by any person or by garages to the Department of Safety are for the confidential use of the department or other state agencies having use of the records for accident prevention purposes, or for administrating laws relating to the deposit of security and proof of financial responsibility by motor vehicle drivers or owners.[30]

Adoption and foster care records

Records pertaining to the final order of adoption or the final order dismissing adoption proceedings are sealed and can be opened only by a court order. The state statute directs that agencies must forward all adoption records to the department of human services for safekeeping.[31]

Records used to compile the Department of Human Services annual report[32] on foster care and records used in the process of placing a child[33] in foster care are confidential.

Attorneys: misconduct by or disability

Proceedings involving allegations of misconduct by or the disability of an attorney are confidential until and unless a recommendation for the imposition of public discipline is filed with the Supreme Court by the Board of Professional Responsibility or the respondent-attorney requests that the matter be public, or the investigation is predicated upon conviction of the respondent-attorney for a crime. In addition, the Board shall transmit notice of all public discipline imposed by the Supreme Court on an attorney or the transfer to inactive status due to disability of an attorney to the National Discipline Data Bank maintained by the American Bar Association.[34]

Banks and financial institutions

The Tennessee General Assembly has passed several statutes that make confidential certain records concerning banks and financial institutions. The types of records closed under these statutes are as follows:

- Reports of investigation and examination of the issuers of money orders and all correspondence and memoranda concerning such investigation.[35]
- Information obtained by the commissioner of financial institutions or any bank examiner in making an examination into the affairs of a bank.[36]
- Information obtained by the commissioner affecting changes in the control of banks,[37] including, but not limited to, the following:
    - identity, personal history, business background and experience, and financial condition of each person applying to gain control,
    - a description of the managerial resources and future prospects of each acquiring party,
    - a description of any material pending legal or administrative proceedings in which the applicant is a party,
    - the terms and conditions of any proposed acquisition,
    - the manner in which the acquisition is to be made
    - the identity, source, and amount of the funds or other consideration borrowed or otherwise obtained for the purpose of making the acquisition,
    - a description of the transaction,
    - the names of the parties, and
    - arrangements, agreements, or understanding with such persons;
    - plans or proposals that an acquiring party may have to liquidate the bank, to sell its assets or merge it with any company, or to make any other major changes in its business or corporate structure or management;

Records submitted by the commissioner of financial institutions to county district attorneys general or to the Tennessee Bureau of Investigation concerning criminal violations of banking laws are confidential and do not become a matter of public record by virtue of such communication.[38]

Civil service and achievement tests and answers

Department of Personnel civil service tests and answers[39] and student achievement tests and answers[40] are exempt from the public records act "for so long as necessary to protect the integrity of the tests."

Claims against the state

For claims against the state, the part of the Division of Claims Administration records containing the amount of funds reserved for each claim for the claims award fund is not subject to the open records act until the final adjudication of the claim. The availability of state records and documents concerning claims are subject to the same discovery defenses as are available to other parties.[41]

Community grant agency: reports of improper actions by employees

Detailed information received by the comptroller concerning improper actions by employees of community grant agencies are considered working papers of the comptroller and therefore confidential. The comptroller's office is required to include in its annual report a summary of the calls received during the year, the general nature of the activities reported, the community grant agencies and state agencies affected and, if appropriate, any remedial action taken or proposed.[42]

Confidential communications between professionals and their clients

The General Assembly has passed statutes that make privileged the confidential relations and communications between some professionals and their clients. Such communications are not only exempt from the public records act, but they are also unavailable for court subpoena or for discovery proceedings.

The professions include as follows:

- certified master social worker, or an independent practitioner of social work holding a valid certificate or registration (except for mandatory child abuse reports);[43]

- licensed psychologists and psychological examiners (except for mandatory child abuse reports);
- psychiatrists;[44]
- certified marital and family therapists or licensed professional counselors (except for mandatory child abuse reports);[45]

Also privileged are all information, interviews, incident or other reports, statements, memoranda or other data furnished to medical review committees and any findings, conclusions or recommendations resulting from the proceedings of such committees. This privilege does not extend to records made in the regular course of business by a hospital or other provider of health care and information, documents or records otherwise available from original sources.[46]

Department of Agriculture health certificates

Official health certificates, collected and maintained by the state veterinarian of the department of agriculture are confidential.[47]

Dispositional reports on juveniles

A court may order that in any case or class of cases a predisposition report should be made, including an investigation and evaluation of the habits, surroundings, conditions and tendencies of a child. The report shall be made by the youth services officer, probation officer, or other person designated by the court. Generally, the child, his attorney, and his parent, guardian or legal custodian shall be entitled to inspect the predisposition report and all medical, psychological and other reports on which it is based, except that information protected from disclosure by law.[48]

Election law violations

Records concerning investigations conducted by the coordinator of elections of reported election law violations are not subject to the public records act.[49]

Employment security laws

Information obtained by the Department of Employment Security while enforcing employment security laws is confidential in accordance with regulations described in the federal Social Security Act.[50] However, documents, records, affidavits, testimony or other information introduced into the record at any hearing before an appeals referee or the board of review is not confidential unless expressly prohibited by other state or federal law or by administrative or judicial protective order. Hearings before an appeals referee or the board of review will be open to the public, subject to such rules as the board of review may prescribe in accordance with the provisions of the Uniform Administrative Procedures Act and applicable federal law.[51]

Expunged arrest records

Tennessee law provides that a person who has been charged with a crime may petition to have the records regarding the charge to be removed and destroyed if one of the following conditions exist: if the charge is dismissed, if no true bill is returned by a grand jury, if a diversion program is successfully completed, if a verdict of not guilty is returned by a jury or if a conviction is reversed on appeal.[52]

The statute providing for expungement of arrest records states that the term "public records," for the purpose of expunction only, does not include arrest histories, investigative reports, law enforcement intelligence information, or files of district attorneys general that are maintained as confidential records for law enforcement purposes and are not open for public inspection or confidential records of the department of human services that are required to be maintained by state or federal law for audit or other purposes.[53]

In several instances law enforcement officials have refused access to records on the basis of the expungement statute. In 1984, for example, a reporter for the Memphis Commercial Appeal sought to inspect the file of a completed Memphis Police Department investigation of a incident in which seven occupants of a house were killed in a shoot-out with police. The Tennessee Supreme Court affirmed the rulings of two lower courts in denying the police department argument that the closed file should be withheld from public scrutiny. The court held that the definition of public records contained in the expungement statute is limited to the purpose of expunction only and that, in the case at hand, no expunction order had been entered that was relevant to the records sought.[54]

In the same case, the court rejected the argument that a provision[55] of the Tennessee Rules of Criminal Procedure exempted police records from disclosure. The court held that Rule 16 applied only to discovery in criminal cases, not to closed files where no pending or contemplated criminal action existed.[56]

The Tennessee Supreme Court has also held that the expungement statute does not violate the separation of powers provisions, ruling that control of the use of such records is properly a legislative, not judicial function.[57]

Financial and tax records

Tax returns and records in the possession of the commissioner of revenue are confidential.[58] Taxpayer statements, reports, returns, and audits are closed to the public,[59] as is certain property tax information furnished to local authorities.[60]

The commissioner of revenue is empowered to prescribe how much and what portion of records concerning gift taxes[61] and inheritance taxes[62] are open to the public and may exchange information with the United States government or with other state governments.

Financial information submitted to the Collection Services Board by applicants for, or holders of, professional, business, or trade licenses[63] and to the Board for Licensing Contractors by contractors[64] is confidential.

Information that would identify an owner of a public obligation is not open to public inspection although such information might be in the possession of banks, trust companies, financial institutions or other financial intermediaries of the issuer, including, but not limited to, registration, paying or transfer agents.[65]

The records of savings and loan associations are confidential except under specified circumstances.[66]

Hazardous waste reduction progress reports

Progress reports submitted to comply with the Hazardous Waste Reduction Act are not public records.[67] The act directed that large quantity generators should complete the first annual progress report on or before March 1, 1993. Small-quantity generators were told to complete the first annual progress report on or before March 1, 1995.

Hospitals: reports to joint commission on accreditation

All hospitals and nursing homes licensed by the department of health that have obtained accreditation from the joint commission on accreditation of hospitals are required to remit licensing fees each year and a copy of a letter of current accreditation and accompanying report from the joint commission on accreditation of hospitals. This report is a confidential record.[68]

Inmate and parolee records

Inmate records are open for public inspection. However, the commissioner of corrections has the authority to delete names of and identifying information about department employees, law enforcement officers, informants or other inmates if, in the commissioner's opinion, public disclosure would jeopardize the safety of those people. If the commissioner determines that a name or identifying information cannot be deleted sufficiently to protect any such person, the commissioner may refuse to disclose the entire document.[69]

The state Parole Board keeps social, physical, mental, psychiatric and criminal information for every prisoner released under its supervision, including reports of parole officers. The board has the authority to make rules concerning the privacy of such records and of the records of its employment bureau.[70]

Insurance information

When a borrower is required to keep real estate insured and to furnish evidence of such insurance to a lender as a condition for obtaining or keeping the loan, then the lender, mortgagee, assignee, or creditor is prohibited from disclosing information about the expiration dates of the policy or other policy information without the written consent of the policyholder.[71]

Also confidential are information concerning a change in control of an insurer[72] and the identity of a lender for merger or acquisition of control of an insurance holding company.[73]

Reports made by insurance companies to the state board of medical examiners concerning the settlement of medical negligence or malpractice claims are not subject to the open records act.[74]

Records of the insurer and other documents concerning a delinquency proceeding by the commissioner of commerce and insurance against a domestic insurer are closed to the public.[75] The commissioner may file in the chancery court of Davidson County a petition seeking a court order for a formal delinquency proceeding against an insurer, and an insurer subject to such an order has the right to petition the court for a hearing and review of the order to be held privately in chambers.[76] The commissioner may open the proceedings or hearings or make public the notices, correspondence, reports, records or other information if the commissioner deems that it is in the best interest of the public or in the best interest of the insurer, its insureds, creditors or the general public.[77]

Investigative records

Tennessee Bureau of Investigation: Investigative records of the Tennessee Bureau of Investigation are closed to public inspection.[78] This includes criminal history information, commonly known as "rap sheets."

TBI investigative records are available to state governmental agencies for the limited purpose of determining whether a license or permit should be issued to a party engaged in an authorized activity affecting the rights, property or interests of the public.

Attorney General's Office: Books, records and other materials in the possession of the office of the attorney general and reporter that relate to any pending or contemplated legal or administrative proceeding in which the office of the attorney general and reporter may be involved are not be open for public inspection if the material is confidential or privileged by state law, relates to investigations conducted by federal law enforcement or federal regulatory agencies, which are confidential or privileged under federal law.[79]

Also exempt are the work products of the attorney general and reporter or any attorney working under his supervision and control, as well as communications made in the context of the attorney-client relationship. Such information may be disclosed to the public, of course, during the discharge of the duties of the office of the attorney general.[80]

All testimony, books, documents, or other writings, records or tangible objects obtained by the attorney general to carry out his or her investigative authority are confidential.[81]

The legislature has specifically stated that books, records and other materials in the possession of other departments are open, even though copies of the same documents also in the possession of the attorney general's office are not subject to inspection or copying in that office.[82]

Pending criminal action: In the 1986 case *Memphis Publishing Co. v. Holt*,[83] the Tennessee Supreme Court ruled that once a police department investigation became inactive, it was open for public inspection. The court's rationale for its decision was based in part on the fact that municipal police department investigative files, unlike TBI and various other investigative files, were not listed among the numerous statutes that describe records as being confidential or among the exemptions identified in the Open Records Act itself.[84] This ruling has allowed journalists and other members of the public to gain access to law enforcement information about criminal investigations that are no longer active, but it has no bearing on investigations of pending cases or on investigative files that the General Assembly has specifically exempted from the state Open Records Act.

Tennessee Rules of Criminal Procedure provide that investigative records relevant to a pending or contemplated criminal actions are not open the public.[85] In a 1987 case, the Tennessee Supreme Court held that the records concerning an investigation into the death of an inmate in a state correctional facility were closed under Rule 16 because the records were relevant to a pending criminal prosecution.[86]

Criminal investigative files of the motor vehicle enforcement division of the department of safety relating to stolen vehicles or parts and files of the department of safety relating to bogus drivers' licenses issued to undercover law enforcement agents are also closed.[87]

Investigative records and reports of the internal affairs division of the department of correction or of the department of youth development are closed to the public except with a subpoena or court order.[88]

Information obtained by law enforcement personnel during official polygraph examinations[89] and results of blood tests ordered by a district attorney general on the victim of a fire death are confidential.[90]

Information obtained during private investigations to determine whether the Tennessee Securities Act of 1980 has been violated is confidential.[91]

Also exempt from openness are investigative records of the Tennessee State Racing Commission's security division.[92]

Judges: disability or misconduct

The Court of the Judiciary is authorized to investigate and take appropriate action including removing from office an active judge who is guilty of misconduct or who suffers from any disability, physical or mental, that is or is likely to become permanent and that would substantially interfere with the prompt, orderly and efficient performance of judicial duty. Complaints made to the Court of the Judiciary regarding disabilities[93] or misconduct[94] of judges are confidential and privileged.

Judiciary court business

The Court of the Judiciary[95] has replaced the Judicial Standards Commission and is authorized "to investigate, hear and determine charges sufficient to warrant discipline or removal" of judges.[96] The Court of the Judiciary has the authority[97] to issue opinions as to whether certain conduct does or does not violate a particular canon or canons. These opinions shall be given publicity through normal judicial channels such as the "Tennessee Judge" or similar publications.

Matters that come before the Court of the Judiciary are confidential. Individual members of the Court will not discuss any matter pending before the Court, except with other members.[98]

Juvenile court records

Except for traffic cases, files and records of juvenile courts are closed except to the following people: the judge, officers and professional staff of the court; parties to the proceeding and their counsel and representatives; a public or private agency or institution providing supervision or having custody of the child under order of the court; the court and its probation and other officials or professional staff and the attorney for the defendant for use in preparing a presentence report in a criminal case in which the defendant is convicted and who prior thereto had been a party to the proceeding in juvenile court.[99] In addition, the statute provides that the court may grant access to any other person, agency or institution with a legitimate interest in the proceeding or in the work of the court.

Library users' identities

In 1988, at the request of librarians in the state, the General Assembly passed a law providing that library records that would reveal the identities of people using libraries in the state are not subject to the open records act.[100] The statute applies to any library, even those privately owned, that are open to the public.

Medical records

Hospital records are not considered public records.[101] Further, the medical records of patients in state, county and municipal hospitals or medical facilities or patients who receive treatment, in whole or in part, at public expense are exempt from the open records act. Likewise exempt are records containing the sources[102] of body parts for transplantation and information about transplant donors.[103]

Information submitted to the Department of Health as part of the cancer reporting system that could possibly identify individuals whose medical records have been used for collecting data may not be included in materials available to the public. The commissioner of health, with the advice of an advisory committee, is authorized to make available personally identifiable portions of the data to researchers, provided that specific guidelines are observed.[104]

Records identifying patients or former patients treated for mental illness or mental retardation are confidential.[105]

Also confidential to the extent that they would identify individuals are abortion records,[106] the results of HIV virus tests,[107] medical laboratory reports of infectious diseases,[108] and sexually transmitted diseases,[109] as well as individual medical information collected by or held by health insurance entities.[110]

In 1991 the General Assembly made confidential records of employees' identity, diagnosis, treatment, or referral for treatment through the government employee assistance programs if the records are maintained separately from personnel and other employee records that are open.[111]

Medical personnel: reviews of

Information received by the Board of Veterinary Medical Examiners through inspections and investigations are not disclosed except in a proceeding involving the question of license. However, records concerning granting or denying veterinary licenses are open to public inspection.[112]

Information provided to and the conclusions of Medical Review Committee[113] or Dental Peer Review Committee[114] proceedings are confidential.

Allegations against a practitioner of the healing arts and the various branches thereof compiled during an investigation by the Division of Health and Related Boards are public information upon the filing of notice of charges.[115] However, the identity of a patient and a complainant or witness who requests anonymity are confidential until introduced at the disciplinary proceedings, as are medical records.[116]

Military records

Records, documents and papers in the possession of the military department that involve the security of the United States and/or the state of Tennessee, including, but not restricted to national guard personnel records, staff studies and investigations are exempted from the open records act.[117]

Payroll records

Payroll records submitted to the Department of Labor as required by the Prevailing Wage Act are not open, but other records and documentation provided to the department to comply with the act are public.[118]

State purchases and bids for service contracts

State agency records containing opinions of value of real and personal property intended to be acquired for a public purpose are closed to the public until the acquisition has been finalized. This, of course, does not prohibit a party to a condemnation action from making discovery relative to property values.[119]

Similarly, proposals received for professional and consultant service contracts and sealed bids for the purchase of goods and services, leases of real property, and individual purchase records are closed until the state has completed its evaluation.[120]

Contracts and leases concerning regulation of railways by the Public Service Commission are not subject to the public records act.[121]

Student records

Records of students in public educational institutions are not subject to the open records act. The governing board of the institution, the department of education, and the Tennessee higher education commission have access on a confidential basis to such records as are required to fulfill their lawful functions. Statistical information not identified with a particular student may be released, however, as well as an individual student's name, age, address, dates of attendance, grade levels completed, class placement and academic degrees awarded.[122]

The Tennessee statute exempting student records specifically mentions records "relating to academic performance, financial status of a student or his parent or guardian, medical or psychological treatment or testing."[123] The statute does not prevent reporters or other members of the public from receiving at least some information about crime on campus involving identifiable students either as victims or criminal suspects.

During the late 1980s and early 1990s, journalists throughout the nation frequently were denied access to information about crimes committed on campuses of public colleges and universities if students were involved and if campus police had assumed jurisdiction. As authority to deny access, officials typically cited the Family Educational Rights and Privacy Act (FERPA),[124] a federal statute commonly known as the Buckley Amendment. Under the terms of this act, federal funds can be denied to institutions that released student records without the consent of the student involved or his or her guardians in the case of a minor student.

The federal Department of Education interpreted FERPA to include student records in the possession of a campus security force. In Tennessee, as well as in many other states, journalists often discovered that, unless the local municipal police assumed jurisdiction in a case, the public could not learn the names and other information about either the victims or alleged perpetrators of crimes committed on university property if students were involved.

On the University of Tennessee, Knoxville, campus, for example, the student newspaper waged a battle spanning several years in an effort to gain access to information about crime on the campus. Student editors gained support from local professional media in at least two highly newsworthy campus crimes — a fraternity house murder in 1988 and an alleged rape in the athletic residence hall in 1990.

In November 1991 editors of The University Daily Beacon, joined by the Student Press Law Center and the editor in chief of the student newspaper at Colorado State University, were successful in their lawsuit for a preliminary injunction to prevent the U.S. Department of Education from continuing to use the threatened cutoff of funds as a weapon to prevent the release of campus crime records.[125] The district court judge held that the student editors had "a substantial likelihood of success on the merits of their claim despite the somewhat limited protection that the First Amendment provides the right to receive information."[126] The judge wrote that in cases approving a rule or law restricting public access to information, the Supreme Court has noted a governmental interest justifying the restriction.[127] But, the judge said, in its answer to the suit, the Department of Education had not offered a single justification for preventing universities from disclosing the names of students involved in criminal activity.

In another lawsuit challenging of the Department of Education's restrictive definition of student records, a federal district judge in Missouri held that the Buckley Amendment could not be used as justification to violate the terms of the Missouri open records law and that it was a violation of both Fifth and First amendment rights for a state to withhold criminal incident reports.[128] The Department of Education, headed by Lamar Alexander, former Tennessee governor and former president of the University of Tennessee system, was unsuccessful in its attempts to have the preliminary injunction lifted.

In July 1992, the Higher Education Act Amendments of 1992 became law, including a provision to change the Family Educational Rights and Privacy Act so that campus crime records concerning individual students would be open to the public.[129] If a school combines police records with academic records, the police portion of the record must be open.

Another federal statute affecting public access to information about crime on campus is the Student Right to Know and Campus Security Act of 1990. Beginning on Sept. 1, 1992, the act required colleges and universities that receive federal funds to publish timely reports of the numbers and types of crimes committed on campus.[130]

Trade secrets and proprietary information

The capital plans,[131] marketing information,[132] proprietary information[133] and trade secrets[134] submitted to the Tennessee venture capital network at Middle Tennessee State University are exempt from the open records act.[135]

Information containing trade secrets that is filed with the commissioner of labor in compliance with the Hazardous Chemical Right to Know Law is exempt from the public records act. The legislature has also mandated that administrative hearings and judicial proceedings relative to enforcement of the Hazardous Chemical Right to Know Law are also closed to the public.[136]

Information defined as proprietary by regulation and that is supplied to the Department of Health and Environment pursuant to the Atomic Energy and Nuclear Materials Act is confidential.[137]

Also confidential by Tennessee statute are documentary material, merchandise, or other information, including trade secrets, requested by the Consumer Affairs Division in its enforcement of the Consumer Protection Act of 1977.[138]

The office of the commissioner of labor is prohibited by statute from revealing trade secrets submitted to the office as required for enforcement of the Occupational Safety and Health Act.[139]

Information obtained by or reported to the commissioner of labor pursuant to state occupational safety and health laws[140] is exempt from the public records act.

In 1991 the Tennessee General Assembly made confidential records or materials that contain proprietary information,[141] trade secrets[142] or patentable materials[143] received, generated, ascertained or discovered during sponsored research[144] conducted within public higher education institutions in the state.[145] The legislature mandated that in order to qualify as closed, the records or material must be so designated by the chancellor of the Tennessee board of regents system or the president of the University of Tennessee system. The chancellor or president may not close these records without specifying that the research could not proceed if open to the public, and that continuing the research is in the best interest of the institution and the state. Then, before such records can become confidential , the attorney general and reporter must affirmatively agree with the designation made by either university official. The statute provides, however, that the public higher education institution must reveal, upon request, the title, description, the amount and source of funding of a sponsored research project.

A 1983 state statute makes confidential any information submitted to or compiled by the Tennessee Competitive Export Corporation in connection with its responsibilities with respect to the identity, background, finance, marketing plans, trade secrets or any other commercially sensitive information of persons, firms, associations, partnerships, agencies, corporations or other entities unless the person or entity that provided such information consents to disclosure.[146]

The commissioner of economic and community development and the state attorney general have the authority to designate that proprietary information held by the Department of Economic and Community Development is confidential.[147]

Information obtained by the board or commissioner *except* secret formulae or proprietary manufacturing processes pursuant to the Water Quality Control Act is available to the public for reasonable inspection and copying.[148]

Information concerning applications to the Oil and Gas Board for permits and the issuance of permits for the drilling of mineral tests holes is proprietary information that is to be kept confidential.[149]

Vital records

An act passed in 1977 and amended in 1988 makes it unlawful for any person to permit inspection of or to disclose information contained in vital records, except the fact and date that a person was born or died. The state registrar has the authority to establish a method whereby a question as to whether and when a person was born or died may be answered without revealing any details of such birth or death.[150]

One hundred years after the date of birth or fifty years after the date of death, marriage, divorce, dissolution of marriage or annulment, the records of these events in the custody of the state registrar become public records.[151]

Tennessee newspapers commonly publish lists of births, deaths, marriages and divorces after receiving such information from county clerks and other sources. An opinion released by the state attorney general in June 1992 called attention to this exception to the state Open Records Act, causing some county clerks to reassess their practice of releasing such information and sparking journalists to call for legislation to grant access to vital records.[152]

Welfare recipients

Lists of welfare recipients submitted to the Department of Human Services may not be used for political or commercial purposes and no one is permitted to copy a list.[153] The list, name or any other information concerning identifiable persons who apply for or receive aid to families with dependent children[154] or food stamps[155] are not subject to the open records act.

Work papers in certain General Assembly offices

All books, papers, records, and correspondence of the Office of Legal Services[156] and the Office of Program Development[157] pertaining to their work are public records except:

- Intra-office memoranda made by the directors and their staffs; and
- Work papers and correspondence with any person receiving service from the office of legal services.

In addition, material supplied to the Office of Program Development by a state or local government agency or department that under applicable law would remain confidential in the hands of that agency or department is also confidential if held by the Office of Program Development. Further, the office has the authority to withhold from the public record any information supplied to it by a committee or member of the general assembly who requests confidentiality.

Papers and correspondence of either the Legal Services or Program Development offices may become public records if so ordered by the general assembly or the head of the office holding the material.

How are confidential records handled?

The section of the statute dealing with confidential records directs that in their maintenance, storage and disposition, agencies are to treat such records as confidential and that such "records shall be destroyed in such a manner that they cannot be read, interpreted or reconstructed. The destruction shall be in accordance with an approved records disposition authorization from the public records commission.[158]

The following subsection, however, specifies that any confidential public record in existence more than 70 years shall be open for public inspection unless disclosure of the record is specifically prohibited or restricted by federal law or unless the record is a record of services for a person for mental illness or mental retardation. The provisions of this section do not apply to a record concerning an adoption or a record maintained by the office of vital records or by the Tennessee Bureau of Investigation.[159]

Some Examples from Attorney General Opinions

The following is a partial list of materials that, according to opinions of the Tennessee Attorney General during the past several years, are open for public inspection:

- lists of election officials; (OAG 83-404)
- orders from administrative hearings; (OAG 84-104)
- eligibles on a civil service list and where an applicant stands relative to others on the list; (OAG 80-125)
- voter registration list; (OAG 80-497)
- payroll information maintained by a municipal school system; (OAG 90-15)
- names of occupants of residential units paying utility bills; (OAG 84-042)
- maps of a utility division, department, or district concerning its services, even if such maps are not required by law to be maintained; (OAG 86-098)
- records of limited guardianship proceedings, after adjudication, including pleadings, orders, and psychiatrists' affidavits; (OAG 87-140)

- housing development proposals submitted to the Tennessee Housing Development Agency; (OAG 83-75)
- decision books, minute books, and docket books of the Board of Review of the Department of Employment Security; (OAG 82-289).
- an evaluation report of a school superintendent conducted by school board members pursuant to law or in connection with the transaction of official business; (OAG 82-37)
- campaign financial disclosure reports. The Secretary of State or County Election Commission must record name and address of person inspecting the records and notify the candidate within thirty days. (OAG 89-112)

The Tennessee Court of Appeals has held that personnel files of applicants for the position of school superintendent were public records in the hands of a search committee.[160]

Attorney General opinions have considered the following records to be exempt from the public records act:

- records of the Tennessee Student Assistance Corp. concerning student loans in default; (OAG 82-103)
- reports relating to individual banks as compiled by the Department of Property Assessment for calculating bank excise tax distributions to local jurisdictions if those reports are comingled with confidential tax information; (OAG 83-465)
- confidential records transferred to State Archives; (OAG 84-029)
- work sheets compiled by the Public Service Commission containing salaries of public utility employees that have not been introduced into the record in a pending case; (OAG 82-363)
- evaluations of school principals conducted under the Career Ladder Program. (OAG 91-108)

Access to Federal Information

The Freedom of Information Act, passed by Congress in 1966 and amended several times, provides that all records in the possession of agencies of the federal government must be disclosed unless they are specifically exempt.[161]

What Agencies Are Subject to the FOI Act?

The FOIA defines agency as "each authority of the Government of the United States, whether or not it is within or subject to review by another agency.[161] This includes any executive department, military department, government corporation, government controlled corporation, or other establishment in the executive branch of the government (including the Executive Office of the president), or any independent regulatory agency.[162]

The act does not include the president and his immediate personal White House staff, Congress, the courts, governments of the territories or possessions of the United States or the District of Columbia, courts martial and military commissions or military authority exercised in the field in time of war or in occupied territory.

What Records Are Included?

This question has been the subject of numerous court cases since the act was originally passed. Generally, the term is defined expansively to include all types of documentary information, such as papers, reports, letters, films, computer tapes, photographs, and sound recordings. It does not include physical items, such as the rifle used in the assassination of President John F. Kennedy.

The act does not apply to records of state or local governments; however, information submitted to a federal agency by a state or local agency or by the courts or Congress becomes subject to the FOIA if a federal agency has *control* over the records and if the record does not fall into one of the nine exempt categories. Note, however, that not all records in the *possession* of a federal executive branch agency, such as those from state or local governments or Congress, are necessarily under the control of the federal agency and thus subject to disclosure under the FOIA.

Using the Freedom of Information Act

Who may use it?

The statute provides for access to "any person," which has been interpreted to mean organizations, corporations and foreign nations, among others. A person's citizenship or purpose for wanting the information are immaterial.

How are requests made?

Persons seeking to gain access to a particular record through the FOIA do not have to know the specific number or name of the document, but they must be able to "reasonably describe" the material they want, and they must know what agency has the material. The Federal Register is helpful here because each agency is required to publish the following in the Register:

- "descriptions of its central and field organization and the established places at which, the employees (and in the case of a uniformed service, the members) from whom, and the methods whereby, the public may obtain information, make submittals or requests, or obtain decisions"[164];
- "statements of the general course and method by which its functions are channeled and determined, including the nature and requirements of all formal and informal procedures available"[165];
- "rules of procedure, descriptions of forms available or the places at which forms may be obtained, and instructions as to the scope and contents of all papers, reports, or examinations"[166];
- "substantive rules of general applicability adopted as authorized by law, and statements of general policy or interpretations of general applicability formulated and adopted by the agency"[167]; and
- "each amendment, revision, or repeal of the foregoing."[168]

Material that does not have to be published in the Federal Register is also available for public inspection. The FOIA requires that each agency make available the following:

- those statements of policy and interpretations which have been adopted by the agency and are not published in the Federal Register;[169]
- administrative staff manuals and instructions to staff that affect a member of the public; unless the materials are promptly published and copies offered for sale. To the extent required to prevent a clearly unwarranted invasion of personal privacy, an agency may delete identifying details

when it makes available or publishes an opinion, statement of policy, interpretation, or staff manual or instruction. However, in each case the justification for the deletion shall be explained fully in writing.

- current indexes providing identifying information for the public as to any matter issued, adopted, or promulgated after July 4, 1967, and required by this paragraph to be made available or published. Each agency shall promptly publish, quarterly or more frequently, and distribute (by sale or otherwise) copies of each index or supplements thereto unless it determines by order published in the Federal Register that the publication would be unnecessary and impracticable, in which case the agency shall nonetheless provide copies of such index on request at a cost not to exceed the direct cost of duplication.[170]

The United States Government Manual can also help pinpoint which agency may have the documents sought. If you are still uncertain, call or write the public affairs or FOA offices of those agencies you think may have the material to determine where to send your written request for specific records. Local or regional offices, rather than the agency headquarters, may have the material you seek. Generally, the central office has control over policy-related and general information, and the field offices possess working files.

It is advisable to work through the public affairs officer for an agency because they are accustomed to dealing with the media and requests for records. It is also recommended that you keep a copy of all correspondence and record of telephone conversations concerning your FOIA requests.

How much does it cost to use the FOI act?

If records are requested by a representative of the news media or an educational or noncommercial scientific institution, whose purpose is scholarly or scientific research, the FOIA provides that no charges are made for the first two hours of search time or for the first one hundred pages of duplication. Fees for additional time or pages are limited to reasonable standard charges for document duplication, with no costs assessed for time spend searching and reviewing the records.[171] News media and researchers may be able to get fees waived entirely or reduced if "disclosure of the information is in the public interest because it is likely to contribute significantly to public understanding of the operations or activities of the government and is not primarily in the commercial interest of the requester."[172]

People making requests for commercial use are expected to pay for search and review[173] time as well as duplication costs.[174] For requests that are unrelated to news media, research, or commercial purposes, the fees are for search and duplication.[175]

Agencies may not require advance payment of fees unless the requester has previously failed to pay fees in a timely fashion, or the agency has determined that the fee will exceed $250.[176]

What is the time frame for complying with requests?

For journalists working on a tight deadline, the FOIA is generally not helpful because agencies have ten days (excepting Saturdays, Sundays, and legal public holidays) after receiving a request to decide whether to comply with the request. If the agency decides that the information sought is outside the scope of the FOIA or is exempt, the agency must immediately notify the person making the request, give reasons for the denial, and information about appealing the decision.[177]

Even if there is no dispute about the openness of records, the material is rarely delivered to the requester within ten working days. The sheer volume of requests prevents speedy compliance in most situations.

In "unusual circumstances" an agency has an additional ten working days to determine whether a request will be granted. "Unusual circumstances," as defined by the FOIA, includes "the need to search for and collect the requested records from field facilities or other establishments that are separate from the office processing the request; the need to search for, collect, and appropriately examine a voluminous amount of separate and distinct records which are demanded in a single request; or the need for consultation, which shall be conducted with all practicable speed, with another agency having a substantial interest in the determination of the request or among two or more components of the agency having substantial subject-matter interest therein."[178]

How are denials appealed?

If an agency denies a request for information, it must notify the requester and specify the reason for the denial. The requester has the right to appeal the decision to the agency, which then must act on the appeal within twenty working days.[179]

If the request is again denied in whole or in part, the agency must notify the requester of the provisions for judicial review. The notice should also indicate the names and titles or positions of each person responsible for the denial.

Once administrative remedies are exhausted, the requester has the right to file suit with a federal district court in his home district, where the agency records are situated, or in the District of Columbia. The defendant agency then has thirty days to file an answer with the court.[180]

The district court has the authority to examine the contents of the record privately to determine whether it falls into one of the categories exempt from the FOIA.[181] The burden of proof is on the agency.

Are penalties assessed for improper withholding?

If the court determines that the records were improperly withheld, it may assess the government with attorney fees and other litigation costs.[180]

Furthermore, if the court finds that the circumstances surrounding the withholding raise questions about whether agency personnel acted arbitrarily or capriciously, the Special Counsel must promptly investigate to determine whether disciplinary action is warranted against the officer or employee primarily responsible for the withholding. The Special Counsel is empowered to make recommendations to the administrative authority, which is compelled to take the corrective action that the Special Counsel recommends.[183]

What records are exempt from the FOI act?

The Freedom of Information Act exempts from disclosure the following categories of matters:[184]

(1) (A) specifically authorized under criteria established by an Executive order to be kept secret in the interest of national defense or foreign policy and (B) are in fact properly classified pursuant to such Executive order;

(2) related solely to the internal personnel rules and practices of an agency;

(3) specifically exempted from disclosure by statute, provided that such statute (A) requires that the matters be withheld from the public in such a manner as to leave no discretion on the issue, or (B) establishes particular criteria for withholding or refers to particular types of matters to be withheld;

(4) trade secrets and commercial or financial information obtained from a person and privileged or confidential;

(5) inter-agency or intra-agency memorandums or letters which would not be available by law to a party other than an agency in litigation with the agency;

(6) personnel and medical files and similar files the disclosure of which would constitute a clearly unwarranted invasion of personal privacy;

(7) records or information compiled for law enforcement purposes, but only to the extent that the production of such law enforcement records or information

  (A) could reasonably be expected to interfere with enforcement proceedings, (If the investigation or proceeding involves a possible violation of criminal law; and there is reason to believe that (i) the subject of the investigation or proceeding is not aware of its pendency, and (ii) disclosure of the existence of the records could reasonably be expected to interfere with enforcement proceedings, the agency may, during only such time as that circumstance continues, treat the records as not subject to the FOIA.)

  (B) would deprive a person of a right to a fair trial or an impartial adjudication,

  (C) could reasonably be expected to constitute an unwarranted invasion of personal privacy,[185]

  (D) could reasonably be expected to disclose the identity of a confidential source, including a state, local, or foreign agency or authority or any private institution which furnished information on a confidential basis, and, in the case of a record or information compiled by criminal law enforcement authority in the course of a criminal investigation or by an agency conducting a lawful national security intelligence investigation, information furnished by a confidential source,

(E) would disclose techniques and procedures for law enforcement investigations or prosecutions, or would disclose guidelines for law enforcement investigations or prosecutions if such disclosure could reasonably be expected to risk circumvention of the law, or

(F) could reasonably be expected to endanger the life or physical safety of any individual;

(8) contained in or related to examination, operating, or condition reports prepared by, on behalf of, or for the use of an agency responsible for the regulation or supervision of financial institutions; or

(9) geological and geophysical information and data, including maps, concerning wells.

Any reasonable segregable portion of a record shall be provided after deletion of the portions that are exempt.

Whenever a request involves access to records maintained by the Federal Bureau of Investigation pertaining to foreign intelligence or counterintelligence, or international terrorism, and the existence of the records is classified information, the Bureau may, as long as the existence of the records remains classified information, treat the records as not subject to the requirements of this section.[186] The exemptions in the FOIA do not give agencies the authority to withhold information from Congress.[187]

Access in the Computer Era

The availability of government-held data in machine-readable format enables journalists to analyze that data in ways that were virtually impossible before computers entered newsrooms. The results have been prize-winning series of articles on topics important to understanding or changing public policy.

Ironically, the powerful new systems designed to store, process, and retrieve vast amounts of data may thwart public access to government information. Increasingly, electronic record keeping is replacing paper, so unless all levels of government develop policies that enable the public to gain access to those computer files, open records acts may become useless.

In an article titled "The Freedom of Information Act in the Electronic Age: The Statute Is Not User Friendly,"[188] Jamie A. Grodsky, a former attorney in the Office of Technology Assessment, identified these four principal unresolved issues concerning access to electronic information under the FOIA:

- To meet the demands of FOIA, an agency does not have to create new records to fulfill requests. Is entering codes into a computer the equivalent of "creating a new record" and thus not required as part of the FOIA search process?
- FOIA says that an agency must exert a "reasonable" amount of effort to respond to requests. How much effort is reasonable? The definitional problems that exist in dealing with paper records are compounded when dealing with electronic records.
- Should agencies be required to provide information in electronic or machine-readable form if the information exists in that form, or do printouts comply with FOIA?
- Should government electronic mail, computer programs, online databases and integrated software and database programs be defined as records and thus available under FOIA?

These are some of the questions that are appearing in the case law. However, the case law thus far is limited, conflicting, or too vague to give consistent direction. Even in those areas where the case law is clear, a 1989 Justice Department survey[189] of agencies subject to the FOIA reveals that agency practice varies widely.

On the state level, the Tennessee General Assembly has mandated that for public information stored in a computer-readable form, the joint legislative services committee has exclusive authority to determine the form in which the information will be reproduced for the requestor of the information and that "if access to such public information is also available in printed form, it need not be provided in an electronic readable form."[190]

This means that journalists and others wishing to use data contained in records subject to the Tennessee public records act may be unable to perform simple statistical analyses without first keystroking that data into a computer, a time-consuming task that would preclude many news organizations from pursuing stories based on such data. An agency would comply with the public records act by making the data available in printed form and refusing to supply it in machine-readable form.

According to an opinion of the state attorney general, information contained in a computer but not yet been printed is subject to the open records act because a printed copy can be made.[191] Another attorney general opinion states that if information in a public record is also stored in a computer, the public records act does not require operation of the computer for purposes of public inspection.[192]

Tennessee law mandates that "the joint legislative services committee shall consider each application for direct access to the legislative computer system in which confidential information is stored or processed, or that is connected to another computer in which confidential information is stored or processed, and solely shall determine whether or not to permit direct access by the applicant."[193] Further, direct access to such a computer may not be permitted unless protection of any confidential information is ensured.[194]

Endnotes

1. T.C.A. 10-7-503(a).

2. T.C.A. 4-5-218.

3. T.C.A. 4-5-218(d).

4. OAG 86-098, quoting 66 Am.Jur.2d Records and Recording Laws §19 (1973).

5. T.C.A. 10-7-505(a).

6. 10-7-505(c). See also, Memphis Publishing Company v. Holt, 701 S.W. 2d 513 (1986).

7. T.C.A. 10-7-505(b).

8. T.C.A. 10-7-505(d).

9. Ibid.

10. T.C.A. 10-7-505(e).

11. Memphis Publishing Co. v. Holt, 710 S.W. 2d 513 (Tenn. 1986).

12. T.C.A. 10-7-505(g).

13. T.C.A. 10-7-505(f).

14. T.C.A. 10-7-503(a).

15. Title 4, chapter 5.

16. T.C.A. 10-7-503(b).

17. Memphis Publishing Company v. Holt, 701 S.W. 2d 513 at 517 (1986), citing Cavender v. Hewitt, 145 Tenn. 471, 475, 239 S.W. 767, 768 (1922).

18. T.C.A. 8-3-104.

19. T.C.A. 10-7-504.

20. T.C.A. 10-7-504.

21. State v. Fears, 659 S.W. 2d 370 (Tenn. Crim. App. 1983), cert. denied, 465 U.S. 1082, 104 S. Ct. 1450, 79 L. Ed. 2d 768 (1984).

22. T.C.A. 37-1-612.

23. Ibid. at(c).

24. Ibid.

25. Ibid.

26. T.C.A. 37-1-409(a)(1).

27. T.C.A. 37-1-409(a)(2).

28. T.C.A. 37-1-403.

29. T.C.A. 71-6-118.

30. T.C.A. 55-10-114.

31. T.C.A. 36-1-129.

32. T.C.A. 37-2-411.

33. T.C.A. 37-2-408.

34. Tennessee Sup.Ct.Rules, Rule 9, Code of Judicial Conduct.

35. T.C.A. 45-7-117.

36. T.C.A. 45-2-1603.

37. T.C.A. 45-2-103.

38. T.C.A. 45-2-1717.

39. T.C.A. 8-30-303.

40. T.C.A. 49-1-302, 49-6-6001.

41. T.C.A. 9-8-307.

42. T.C.A. 8-4-404.

43. T.C.A. 63-23-107.

44. T.C.A. 24-1-207.

45. T.C.A. 63-22-114.

46. T.C.A. 63-6-219. As used in this section, "medical review committee" or "committee" means any committee of state or local professional association or society, or a committee of any licensed health care institution, or the medical staff thereof, or any committee of a medical care foundation or health maintenance organization, preferred provider organization, individual practice association or similar entity, the function of which, or one (1) of the functions of which, is to evaluate and improve the quality of health care rendered by providers of health care service or to determine that health care services rendered were professionally indicated or were performed in compliance with the applicable standard of care or that the cost of health care rendered was considered reasonable by the providers of professional health care services in the area and includes a committee functioning as a utilization review committee under the provisions of Public Law 89-97 (42 U.S.C.

§§ 1395-1396 (Medicare Law) or as a utilization and quality control peer review organization under the provisions of the Peer Review Improvement Act of 1982, Public Law 97-248, §§ 141-150, or a similar committee or a committee of similar purpose, to evaluate or review the diagnosis or treatment or the performance or rendition of medical or hospital services which are performed under public medical program of either state or federal design.

47. T.C.A. 10-7-504(10).

48. Tennessee Rules of Juvenile Procedure, Rule 33.

49. T.C.A. 2-11-202.

50. §§(a)(1), §1137(a)(5) and §1137(a)(5)(B). § 1137 of the Social Security Act is codified as 42 U.S.C. § 1320-7.

51. T.C.A. 50-7-701(a)(1).

52. T.C.A. 40-32-101.

53. T.C.A. 40-32-101(b).

54. Memphis Publishing Company v. Holt, 701 S.W. 2d 513 at 517 (1986).

55. Tennessee Rules of Criminal Procedure, Rule 16(a)(2).

56. Memphis Publishing Company v. Holt, 701 S.W. 2d 513 at 517 (1986).

57. Underwood v. State, 529 S.W.2d 45 (Tenn. 1975).

58. T.C.A. 67-1-1702.

59. T.C.A. 67-4-722.

60. T.C.A. 67-5-401.

61. T.C.A. 67-8-109.

62. T.C.A. 67-8-404.

63. T.C.A. 62-20-119.

64. T.C.A. 62-6-124.

65. T.C.A. 9-19-109.

66. T.C.A. 45-3-807, 45-3-814, 45-3-1308.

67. T.C.A. 68-46-306.

68. T.C.A. 68-11-210.

69. T.C.A. 4-6-140.

70. T.C.A. 40-28-119.

71. T.C.A. 47-23-101.

72. T.C.A. 56-11-204.

73. T.C.A. 56-11-203.

74. T.C.A. 56-3-111.

75. T.C.A. 56-9-202.

76. T.C.A. 56-9-504.

77. T.C.A. 56-9-504(d).

78. T.C.A. 10-7-504(2).

79. T.C.A. 10-7-504(5)(A).

80. *Id.*

81. T.C.A. 8-6-407.

82. T.C.A. 10-7-504(5)(A)(v).

83. 710 S.W.2d 513 (Tenn. 1986).

84. *Id.* at 515.

85. Tennessee Rules of Criminal Procedure, Rule 16.

86. Appman v. Worthington, 746 S.W.2d 165.

87. T.C.A. 10-7-504(2).

88.T.C.A. 10-7-504(9).

89. T.C.A. 62-27-124.

90. T.C.A. 38-7-116.

91. T.C.A. 48-2-118.

92. T.C.A. 4-36-210(b)(2).

93. T.C.A. 17-5-303.

94. T.C.A. 17-5-304.

95. See T.C.A.§ 17-5-101 et seq.

96. T.C.A. 17-5-301.

97. Tennessee Sup.Ct.Rules, Rule 10, Code of Judicial Conduct.

98. Tennessee Sup.Ct.Rules, Rule 7, Code of Judicial Conduct.

99. T.C.A. 37-1-153.

100. T.C.A. 10-8-102.

101. T.C.A. 68-11-304.

102. T.C.A. 68-30-111.

103. T.C.A. 10-7-504(1).

104. T.C.A. 68-1-1006.

105. T.C.A. 33-3-104.

106. T.C.A. 39-15-203.

107. T.C.A. 39-13-521.

108. T.C.A. 68-29-107.

109. T.C.A. 68-10-101.

110. T.C.A. 68-1-108.

111. T.C.A. 10-7-504(d). For purposes of this subsection, "employee assistance program" means any program that provides counseling, problem identification, intervention, assessment, or referral for appropriate diagnosis and treatment, and follow-up services to assist employees of such state or local governmental entity who are impaired by health, marriage, drug, alcohol or mental health problems.

112. T.C.A. 63-12-110.

113. T.C.A. 63-6-219.

114. T.C.A. 63-5-131.

115. T.C.A. 63-1-117(b)(1).

116. T.C.A. 63-1-117(b)(2).

117. T.C.A. 10-7-504(3)

118. T.C.A. 12-4-414.

119. T.C.A. 10-7-504(6).

120. T.C.A. 10-7-504(7).

121. T.C.A. 65-3-109.

122. T.C.A. 10-7-504(4).

123. *Id.*

124. 20 U.S.C 1232(g).

125. Student Press Law Center, Lyn D. Schrotberger, Sam G. Cristy, and James C.Brewer, v. Lamar Alexander, Secretary, Department of Education, and United States Department of Education, 778 F.Supp. 1227, 71 Ed.Law Rep. 794, 19 Media L. Rep. 1620 (D.C. District Court, Nov. 21, 1991).

126. Ibid. at 1234, citing Board of Educ. v. Pico, 457 U.S. 853, 867, 102 S.Ct. 2799, 2808, 73 L.Ed.2d 435 (1982); see Kleindienst v. Mandel, 408 U.S. 753, 762-63, 92 S.Ct. 2576, 2581-82, 33 L.Ed.2d 683 (1972); Red Lion Broadcasting Co. v. FCC, 395 U.S. 367 (1969); Thomas v. Collins, 323 U.S. 516, 65 S.Ct. 315, 89 L.Ed. 430 (1945).

127. *Id.*, citing Pell v. Procunier, 417 U.S. at 830-833, 94 S.Ct. at 2808-2810 (prison security); Kleindienst v. Mandell, 408 U.S. at 770, 92 S.Ct. at 2585-86 (plenary authority to exclude aliens).

128. Bauer v. Kincaid, 759 F.Supp. 575, 590-91 (W.D.Mo.1991).

129. Student Press Law Center Report, Vol. 13 (Fall 1992), p. 5.

130. *Id.*

131. Defined as plans, feasibility studies, and similar research and information that will contribute to the identification of future business sites and capital investments.

132. Defined as marketing studies, marketing analyses, and similar research and information designed to identify potential customers and business relationships.

133. Proprietary information means commercial or financial information used either directly or indirectly in the business of any person or company submitting information to the Tennessee venture capital network at Middle Tennessee State University, and which gives such person an advantage or an opportunity to obtain an advantage over competitors who do not know or use such information.

134. Trade secrets mean manufacturing processes, materials used therein, and costs associated with the manufacturing process of a person or company submitting information to the Tennessee venture capital network at Middle Tennessee State University.

135. T.C.A. 10-7-504(11).

136. T.C.A. 50-3-2013.

137. T.C.A. 68-23-217.

138. T.C.A. 47-18-106.

139. T.C.A. 50-3-504.

140. T.C.A. 50-3-914.

141. T.C.A. 49-7-120(a)(2) defines proprietary information as commercial or financial information which is used either directly or indirectly in the business of any person or company submitting information to the public higher education institu-

tion, and which gives such person or company an advantage or an opportunity to obtain an advantage over competitors who do not know or use such information;

142. Under T.C.A. 49-7-120(a)(4), "trade secrets" means manufacturing processes, materials used therein, and costs associated with the manufacturing process of a person or company submitting information to the public higher education institution.

143. T.C.A. 49-7-120(a)(1) defines "patentable materials" as inventions, processes, discoveries or other subject matter which the public higher education institution or the sponsor reasonably believes to be patentable under U.S.C., title 35.

144. T.C.A. 49-7-120(a)(3) defines "sponsored research" as research or analysis conducted pursuant to grants or contracts between the public higher education institution and an external agency or company. It does not include research conducted under an agreement with other agencies of the state of Tennessee, unless such research is a subcontract to a contract with an external agency or company.

145. T.C.A. 49-7-120.

146. T.C.A. 13-27-113.

147. T.C.A. 4-3-712, 4-3-729.

148. T.C.A. 69-3-113.

149. T.C.A. 60-1-504, 60-1-505.

150. T.C.A. 68-3-205.

151. T.C.A. 68-3-205(d).

152. See, e.g., "An overly broad opinion," editorial published by the *Knoxville News-Sentinel*, June 24, 1992.

153. T.C.A. 71-1-118.

154. T.C.A. 71-3-119.

155. T.C.A. 71-5-304.

156. T.C.A. 3-12-105.

157. T.C.A. 3-14-109.

158. T.C.A. 10-7-504(b).

159. T.C.A. 10-7-504(c).

160. Board of Education of Memphis City Schools v. Memphis Publishing Co., 585 S.W.2d 629 (1979).

161. 5 U.S.C. 552.

162. 5 U.S.C. 551.

163. 5 USCA 552(f).

164. 5 USCA 552(a)(1)(A).

165. 5 USCA 552(a)(1)(B).

166. 5 USCA 552(a)(1)(C).

167. 5 USCA 552(a)(1)(D).

168. 5 USCA 551(a)(1)(E).

169. 5 USCA 552(a)(2)(B).

170. 5 USCA 552(a)(2)(C).

171. 5 USCA 552(4)(A)(ii)(I).

172. 5 USCA 552(4)(A)(iii).

173. 5 USCA 552(4)(A)(iv) provides that review costs shall include only the direct costs incurred during the initial examination of a document for the purposes of determining whether it must be disclosed and for the purposes of withholding any portions exempt from disclosure. Review costs may not include any costs incurred in resolving issues of law or policy that may be raised in the course of processing a request.

174. 5 USCA 552(4)(A)(ii)(II).

175. 5 USCA 552(4)(A)(ii)(III).

176. 5 USCA 552(4)(A)(ii)(v).

177. 5 USCA 552(6)(A)(i).

178. 5 USCA 552(6)(B)(i, ii, iii).

179. 5 USCA 552(6)(A)(ii).

180. 5 USCA 552(6)(C).

181. 5 USCA 552(6)(B).

182. 5 USCA 552(6)(E).

183. 5 USCA 552(6)(F).

184. 5 USCA 552(b)(1-9).

185. The U.S. Supreme Court has held that this section exempts FBI criminal history information, commonly known as "rap sheets," from disclosure. U.S. Dept. of Justice v. Reporters Committee For Freedom of Press, 109 S.Ct. 1468, 489 U.S. 749, 103 L.Ed.2d 774 (1989).

186. 5 USCA 552(C)(1)(3).

187. 5 USCA 552(d)

188. 13 *Jurismetric Journal of Law, Science and Technology* 17-51 (Fall 1990).

189. "Agencies Respond to DOJ Computer Survey, 15 *Access Reports* 22 (Nov. 15, 1989). Also available in FOIA UPDATE, Spring/Summer 1990 issue (Part 1) and Fall 1990 (Part 2).

190. T.C.A. 3-10-108(d).

191. O.A.G 80-125A (1980).

192. O.A.G. 80-288 (1980).

193. T.C.A. 3-10-108(a).

194. *Id.* (d).

Access to Government Meetings

Just as public access to governmental records is considered essential in a democratic system of government, the right to observe the process by which governing bodies conduct public business is equally important. Statutes declaring that government meetings will be open, commonly known as "sunshine acts," exist at both the federal and state levels.

Tennessee Public Meetings Act

The General Assembly has declared it to be state policy that the "formulation of public policy and decisions is public business and shall not be conducted in secret."[1] All meetings of any governing body are open to the public at all times, except as provided by the Tennessee Constitution.[2]

Bodies Subject to the Act

As defined by the Tennessee Open Meetings Act, a "governing body" includes the following:

(a) members of any public body that consists of two or more members, with authority to make decisions for or recommendations to a public body on policy or administration;

(b) a community action agency that administers community action programs;

(c) a public body acting as a negotiation committee for collective bargaining purposes and strategy sessions of such negotiation committee;[3]

(d) the board of directors of any nonprofit corporation that contracts with a state agency to receive community grant funds in exchange for rendering specified public services, provided that such funds comprise at least 30 percent of the total annual income of the corporation;[4]

(e) the board of directors of any not-for-profit corporation authorized by Tennessee law to act on behalf of or for the benefit of one or more counties, cities, towns or local governments pursuant to state statutes regarding energy production facilities[5] and resource recovery and solid waste disposal.[6] However, counties with a metropolitan form of government and a population of 400,000 or more are exempt from this provision.[7]

In addition to units covered by the broad definition of "governing body" in the state public meetings act, statutes provide that meetings of the following are open to the public:

- the board of directors of the Tennessee Performing Art Center Management Corporation;[8]
- Labor negotiations between representatives of public employees unions or associations and representatives of the state or local governmental entity except during strategy sessions where either group meets separately;[9]
- election commissions;[10]
- state primary boards;[11]
- hearings or other proceedings conducted before an administrative judge or hearing officer;[12]
- commission on intergovernmental relations;[13]
- state library and archives management board;[14]
- nominating commission for director of the Tennessee Bureau of Investigation;[15]
- school boards negotiating with professional employees' organizations;[16]
- Four Lakes regional industrial development authority;[17]
- regional municipal solid waste authority.[18]

Court decisions have held that local school board meetings[19] and tenure hearings conducted by school boards[20] are open to the public.

Meetings that May Be Closed

The Tennessee Code Annotated lists a number of statutes as cross references to the state public meetings act. Most declare meetings of certain bodies open, but several statutes permit closed meetings.

These meetings are closed by statute:

- labor negotiation strategy sessions of representatives of public employee unions or associations and governmental entity committees meeting separately;[21]
- administrative hearings held pursuant to the Hazardous Chemical Right to Know Law where trade secrets are confidential;[22]
- board meeting at which confidential information from public depositories are discussed;[23]
- deliberations of the Court of the Judiciary regarding charges against a judge. However, other records, actions and proceedings of the court are open after a presiding judge has determined there is "probable cause to believe that the charges [brought against a judge] are not frivolous and unfounded and are within the permissible scope of the court's inquiry" and after these findings have been communicated to the Court of the Judiciary and the judge involved.[24]
- meetings of the Patients Qualification Review Board that certifies patients and doctors as qualified for participation in the program for controlled substances therapeutic research.[25]

In addition to meetings closed by statute, the Tennessee Supreme Court has held that it would be unconstitutional for the open meetings act to prevent public bodies and their attorneys from privately discussing pending litigation.[26] The court's rationale was that the state constitution gives authority to the supreme court, not the legislature, to license and regulate attorneys within the state. The Code of Professional Responsibility promulgated by the Tennessee Supreme Court specifies that attorneys will maintain the confidentiality of their clients.

The court noted that this is a narrow exception and applies only when the public body is a named party in a lawsuit.[27] In fact, for an attorney to engage in private discussions with a public body for any other purpose may violate another section of the Code of Professional Responsibility.[28]

In a 1977 case, the Tennessee Court of Appeals ruled that neither the faculty members of a university unit nor committees composed of faculty members and students created to assist the dean in decision making were governing bodies subject to the open meetings act.[29] Therefore, they could meet privately. The court reasoned that neither deans nor committees created by deans have the authority to create governing policies because that function resides with the university board of trustees.

Definition of Meeting

The statute defines a meeting as any convening of a governing body of a public body for which a quorum is required in order to make a decision or deliberate toward a decision on any matter. A meeting does not include, however, an on-site inspection of a project or program.[30]

A chance meeting of two or more members of a public body is not considered a meeting, but the statute specifies that "no such chance meetings, informal assemblages, or electronic communication shall be used to decide or deliberate public business in circumvention of the spirit or requirements of this part."[31]

Effective in 1990, a new section of the open meetings act statute allows members of boards, agencies and commissions of state government to "participate in either a regular or special meeting by, or conduct the meeting through the use of any means of communication, electronic or otherwise, by which all members participating may simultaneously hear each other and speak to each other during the meeting."[32] Such meetings must conform to all requirements and the spirit of the open meetings act.

This method of attendance is meant to be used only upon a declaration of necessity by the governing body when presence by all members is not possible within the period of time requiring action. Notices required by the act must state that the meeting will be conducted with some persons participating by electronic or other means of communications.[33]

Required Notice and Minutes

Bodies subject to the open meetings act are required to give "adequate" public notice of all regular and special meetings.[34] The statute does not define "adequate," but a 1974 Tennessee Supreme Court decision said, "Adequate public notice means adequate public notice under the circumstances, or such notice based on the totality of the circumstances as would fairly inform the public."[35]

Minutes of all public meetings must be kept and promptly made available to public inspection. Minutes must include, but are not limited to, a list of persons present, all motions, proposals and resolutions offered, the results of any votes taken and a record of individual votes in the event of roll call.[36]

Penalties for Violating the Act

If a governing body meets secretly, any action taken at the meeting is void and of no effect except for actions, otherwise legal, that affect the public debt of the governing body or entity concerned.[37]

How the Act Is Enforced

Any citizen of Tennessee may apply to a state courts with equity jurisdiction, asking that the court issue an injunction, impose penalties and otherwise enforce the open meetings act.[38] The court hearing a challenge based on the Open Meetings Act must file written findings of fact, conclusions of law and final judgments and these must be recorded in the minutes of the body involved.[39] Further, the court shall permanently enjoin any person judged to be in violation from further violations.[40] The court retains jurisdiction over the parties and subject matter for a year from the date of entry, and defendants much file a written report semiannually to the court of their compliance with the Open Meetings Act.[41]

The Federal Open Meetings Act

Congress passed the "Government on the Sunshine Act" in 1976, declaring it "to be the policy of the United States that the public is entitled to the fullest practicable information regarding the decision-making processes of the federal government. It is the purpose of the act to provide the public with such information while protecting the rights of individuals and the ability of the government to carry out its responsibilities."[42]

Agencies and Meetings Subject to the Act

Agencies whose meetings must be open are all that are "headed by a collegial body composed of two or more individual members, a majority of whom are appointed to such position by the president with the advice and consent of the Senate, and any subdivision thereof authorized to act on behalf of the agency;"[43]

(2) The act defines "meeting" as "the deliberations of at least the number of individual agency members required to take action on behalf of the agency where such deliberations determine or result in the joint conduct or disposition of official agency business."[44]

Notice and Minutes Required

At least one week before the meeting, notice of the time, place, and subject matter, whether the meeting is open or closed, and the name and phone number of the official designated by the agency to respond to requests for information about the meeting, must be published in the Federal Register.[45]

For meetings or portion of a meeting closed to the public (except for exemptions 8, 9A or 10 listed below), the agency must maintain a complete transcript or electronic recording. Such minutes must describe all matters discussed and summarize any actions taken, including a description of each view expressed on any item and the record of any roll call vote. All documents considered in connection with any action must also be identified in the minutes.[46]

Copies of transcripts or minutes, or a transcription of such recording disclosing the identity of each speaker, must be furnished to any person at the actual cost of duplication or transcription. The agency must maintain a complete verbatim copy of the transcript, a complete copy of the minutes, or a complete electronic recording of each meeting, or portion of a meeting, closed to the public, for a period of at least two years after such meeting, or until one year after the conclusion of any agency proceeding with respect to which the meeting or portion was held, whichever occurs later.

Meetings Exempt from the Act

Every portion of every meeting of an agency must be open to public observation except where the agency properly determines that such portion or portions of its meeting or the disclosure of such information is likely to:[47]

(1) disclose matters that are (a) specifically authorized under criteria established by an Executive order to be kept secret

in the interests of national defense or foreign policy and (b) in fact properly classified pursuant to such Executive order;

(2) relate solely to the internal personnel rules and practices of an agency;

(3) disclose matters specifically exempted from disclosure by statute, provided that such statute (a) requires that the matters be withheld from the public in such a manner as to leave no discretion on the issue, or (b) establishes particular criteria for withholding or refers to particular types of matters to be withheld;

(4) disclose trade secrets and commercial or financial information obtained from a person and privileged or confidential;

(5) involve accusing any person of a crime, or formally censuring any person;

(6) disclose information of a personal nature where disclosure would constitute a clearly unwarranted invasion of personal privacy;

(7) disclose investigatory records compiled for law enforcement purposes, or information that if written would be contained in such records, but only to the extent that the production of such records or information would:

(A) interfere with enforcement proceedings,

(B) deprive a person of a right to a fair trial or an impartial adjudication,

(C) constitute an unwarranted invasion of personal privacy,

(D) disclose the identity of a confidential source and, in the case of a record compiled by a criminal law enforcement authority in the course of a criminal investigation, or by an agency conducting a lawful national security intelligence investigation, confidential information furnished only by the confidential source,

(E) disclose investigative techniques and procedures, or

(F) endanger the life or physical safety of law enforcement personnel;

(8) disclose information contained in or related to examination, operating, or condition reports prepared by, on behalf of, or for the use of an agency responsible for the regulation or supervision of financial institutions;

(9) disclose information that the premature disclosure of which would:

(A) in the case of an agency that regulates currencies, securities, commodities, or financial institutions, be likely to (i) lead to significant financial speculation in currencies, securities, or commodities, or (ii) significantly endanger the stability of any financial institution; or

(B) in the case of any agency, be likely to significantly frustrate implementation of a proposed agency action, except in any instance where the agency has already disclosed to the public the content or nature of its proposed action, or where the agency is required by law to make such disclosure on its own initiative prior to taking final agency action on such proposal; or

(10) specifically concern the agency's issuance of a subpoena, or the agency's participation in a civil action or proceeding, an action in a foreign court or international tribunal, or an arbitration, or the initiation, conduct, or disposition by the agency of a particular case of formal agency adjudication or otherwise involving a determination on the record after opportunity for a hearing.

Procedure for Closing a Meeting

Before closing a meeting, the general counsel or chief legal officer of the agency must publicly certify that, in his or her opinion, the meeting is eligible for one of the exemptions and must state each relevant exemptive provision.[48]

Meetings are closed as permitted by the exemptions to the Government in the Sunshine Act only when a majority of the entire membership of the agency votes for closure. The vote of each agency member participating in such vote shall be recorded and no proxies shall be allowed.

Whenever any person whose interests may be directly affected by a portion of a meeting requests that the agency close such portion to the public for any of the reasons referred to exemptions 5, 6, or, the agency, upon request of any one member, shall vote by recorded vote whether to close the meeting.

Within one day of any vote taken to close a meeting the agency must make available to the public the vote of each member on the question. If a portion of a meeting is to be closed to the public, the agency must, within one day of the vote taken, make publicly available a full written explanation of its action closing the portion together with a list of all persons expected to attend the meeting and their affiliation.

Challenging Closure

Any person may bring a proceeding in the United States District Court for the District of Columbia to require an agency to comply with the Government in the Sunshine Act. Subject to applicable statute of limitations, any person may bring a proceeding in the United States Court of Appeals for the District of Columbia to set aside agency regulations not in accord with the requirements of the act.

The federal district courts have jurisdiction to enforce the act by declaratory judgment, injunctive relief, or other relief as may be appropriate. Such actions may be brought by any person against an agency prior to, or within 60 days after, the meeting out of which the violation of this section arises, except that if public announcement of such meeting is not initially provided by the agency in accordance with the requirements of this section, such action may be instituted at any time prior to 60 days after any public announcement of such meeting. Such actions may be brought in the district court of the United States for the district in which the agency met or in which the agency in question has its headquarters, or in the District Court for the District of Columbia.

The burden is on the defendant to sustain his action. In deciding such cases the court may examine in camera any portion of the transcript, electronic recording, or minutes of a meeting closed to the public, and may take additional evidence as it deems necessary. The court, having due regard for orderly administration and the public interest, as well as the interests of the parties, may grant equitable relief as it deems appropriate, including granting an injunction against future violations of this section or ordering the agency to make available to the public such portion of the transcript, recording, or minutes of a meeting as is not authorized to be exempt under the act.

The court may assess against any party reasonable attorney fees and other litigation costs reasonably incurred by any other party who substantially prevails in any action brought in accordance with the provisions of the act, except that costs may be assessed against the plaintiff only where the court finds that the suit was initiated by the plaintiff primarily for frivolous or dilatory purposes. In the case of assessment of costs against an agency, the costs may be assessed by the court against the United States.

The Government in the Sunshine Act does not constitute authority to withhold any information from Congress, and does not authorize the closing of any meeting or portion thereof required by any other provision of law to be open.

Endnotes

1. T.C.A. 8-44-101.

2. T.C.A. 8-44-102.

3. T.C.A. 8-44-102(b)(1).

4. T.C.A. 8-44-101(b)(2). This statute provides for these boards of directors to met in closed session to discuss matters concerning confidential doctor-patient relationships, personnel matters or matters required by state or federal law or regulation to be kept confidential. No other matter shall be discussed at such meetings.

5. T.C.A. Title 7, Chapter 54.

6. T.C.A. Title 7, Chapter 58.

7. T.C.A. 8-44-101(b)(3).

8. T.C.A. 8-44-107.

9. T.C.A. 8-44-201.

10. T.C.A. 2-1-113.

11. T.C.A. 2-13-108.

12. T.C.A. 4-5-312.

13. T.C.A. 4-10-105.

14. T.C.A. 10-1-102.

15. T.C.A. 38-6-101.

16. T.C.A. 49-5-611.

17. T.C.A. 64-5-203.

18. T.C.A. 68-31-814.

19. Dorrier v. Dark, 537 S.W.2d 888 (Tenn.) rehearing denied, 540 S.W.2d 658 (Tenn. 1976).

20. Kendall v. Board of Education, 627 F2d 1 (6th Cir. 1980).

21. T.C.A. 8-44-201.

22. T.C.A. 50-3-2013.

23. T.C.A. 9-4-518(f).

24. T.C.A. 17-5-304.

25. T.C.A. 68-52-105.

26. Smith County Education Association v. Anderson, 676 S.W.2d 328 (Tenn. 1984).

27. Ibid. See also, van Kirk v. Board of Mayor & Alderman, 668 S.W.2d 299 (Tenn. Ct. App. 1983).

28. DR 7-102(A)(7) and (8).

29. Fain v. Faculty of College of Law of University of Tennessee, 552 S.W.2d 752.

30. T.C.A. 8-44-102(c).

31. T.C.A. 8-44-102(d).

32. T.C.A. 8-44-108.

33. T.C.A. 8-44-108(d).

34. T.C.A. 8-44-103.

35. Memphis Publishing Co. v. City of Memphis, 513 S.W.2d at 513.

36.T.C.A. 8-44-104.

37. T.C.A. 8-44-105.

38. T.C.A. 8-44-106 (a).

39. Id. (b).

40. Id. (c).

41. Id. (d).

42. 5 U.S.C.A. 552(b).

43. 5 U.S.C.A. 552(b)(a)(1).

44. 5 U.S.C.A. 552(b)(a)(2).

45. 5 U.S.C.A. 552(b)(a)(3) and 5 U.S.C.A. § 552(b)(e)(1) .

46. 5 U.S.C.A. 552(b)(f)(1).

47. 5 U.S.C.A. 552(b)(c).

48. 5 U.S.C.A. 552(f)(1).

Access to Courts and Court Records

The First Amendment rights of a free press have at times conflicted with rights enumerated in the Sixth Amendment designed to guarantee criminal defendants "a speedy and public trial, by an impartial jury." The Tennessee Constitution, Article 1, Section 9, gives the accused similar protections:

> That in all criminal prosecutions, the accused hath the right to be heard by himself and his counsel; to demand the nature and cause of the accusation against him, and to have a copy thereof, to meet the witnesses face to face, to have compulsory process for obtaining witnesses in his favor, and in prosecutions by indictment or presentment, a speedy public trial, by an impartial jury of the County in which the crime shall have been committed, and shall not be compelled to give evidence against himself.

In light of this potential for conflict between media access and protection for the accused, this chapter considers judicial remedies to counter prejudicial publicity, gag orders, access to judicial proceedings and records, steps the media can take if faced with closure of a court proceeding, and the use of photographic and sound equipment in courtrooms.

Judicial Remedies to Counter Prejudicial Publicity

Judges have multiple options to offset the impact of potentially prejudicial publicity before or during a trial. These options include such actions as

- continuances (postponing the trial),
- change of venue,[1]
- voir dire (questioning of potential jurors),
- sequestering the jury or witnesses,
- controlling conduct in the courtroom and

- controlling the activities and expression of trial participants both inside and outside of the courtroom.

In Tennessee appellate courts have considered many requests to overturn convictions based on claims that prejudicial publicity tainted a jury or that a judge improperly denied a motion for a change of venue despite prejudicial publicity. The Tennessee Supreme Court has held that such challenges may be justified if a jury member's opinion as to guilt or innocence was based on news accounts rather than trial testimony.[2] Generally, however, Tennessee courts do not considered routine media coverage of a crime to be prejudicial to the rights of defendants.

In a 1991 murder trial in Coffee County, for example, voir dire revealed that approximately seventy percent of the potential jurors had read or heard something about the case. The Tennessee Supreme Court denied the defendant's argument that he had been denied an impartial jury and that the judge should have ordered a change of venue. Quoting from a U.S. Supreme Court decision,[3] the Tennessee court said, "Qualified jurors need not, however, be totally ignorant of the facts and issues involved. . . . It is sufficient if the juror can lay aside his impression or opinion and render a verdict based on the evidence presented in court."[4]

The Tennessee Rules of Criminal Procedure provide that prospective jurors who admit to having formed opinions shall be dismissed "for cause" unless the judge determines after questioning that they can be impartial.[5] The trial court has discretion to determine impartiality.[6] In addition to challenges for cause, the defense and prosecution each can exercise a limited number of peremptory challenges. The number of peremptory challenges in a capital offense is 15 for the defendant and eight for the prosecution; for an offense punishable by imprisonment for more than one year, each defendant is entitled to eight peremptory challenges while the state has four. For an offense punishable by imprisonment for less than one year or by fine or both, each side is entitled to three peremptory challenges for each defendant.

In affirming the conviction of a murder defendant, the Tennessee Court of Criminal Appeals characterized a series of newspaper articles in a Putnam County newspaper as "irresponsible" and "sensational in nature"[7] and noted that the lengthy process of jury selection had been exacerbated by extensive pretrial publicity. The court concluded, however, that the facts of the death of the murder victim, a four-year-old child, were "themselves sensational because of the very heinous nature of the crime" and that no complaints had been made on appeal as to the accuracy of the news articles. Further, the appeals court found no abuse of discretion in the judge's not ordering a change of venue because, after extensive questioning during voir dire, every juror finally selected for the trial stated that he or she could give the defendant a fair and impartial trial upon the law and evidence.[8]

In a case involving a metropolitan council member's bribery conviction, the Tennessee Court of Criminal Appeals refused to set aside the verdict because of prejudicial publicity because the defendant and his counsel had generated much of the publicity through press conferences and interviews that they initiated.[9]

Gag Orders

On the Media

In attempts to limit prejudicial publicity during a judicial proceeding, judges have issued restrictive orders against publication of certain information. However, since 1976 when the U.S. Supreme Court upheld a state press association challenge of a gag order in a widely publicized case involving the murder of six family members living in a small Nebraska town, courts have been unlikely to resort to direct restraints on publication of material that comes from open court.

In Nebraska Press Association v. Stuart, a unanimous Court, in holding for the press association, said that "prior restraints on speech and publication are the most serious and the least tolerable infringement on First Amendment rights."[10] To restrict or gag the press, the Court said that the trial judge must meet three conditions:

(1) pre-trial publicity would negatively impact the accused right to a fair trial;

(2) alternative judicial remedies, such as change of venue, continuance, voir dire examination, and sequestration of the jury, would not eliminate the effects of prejudicial publicity;

(3) a prior restraint on the media would be effective.

On Trial Participants

While gag orders on the media are now uncommon, the information flow to the media from potential sources may be restricted by the courts. Attorneys in criminal proceedings in federal district courts in Tennessee are prohibited from publicly releasing information that might unduly influence the outcome of the trial.[11] Before the trial they are specifically prohibited from making public statements related to the prior criminal record, confessions or admissions of guilt, the performance on tests or the refusal to be tested, the identity or testimony of prospective witnesses, the likelihood of reduced charges or guilty pleas, or an opinion on the guilt or innocence of the accused. However, attorneys involved in the case may give the facts and circumstances of the arrest, the evidence seized, the nature of the charge, information from public records, and trial scheduling.[12]

During the trial, lawyers for both the defense and prosecution may give only information on the public record, and after the trial, the lawyers may not give information that is likely to unfairly influence sentencing. In a sensational or widely publicized criminal trial, the court may further restrict lawyers from making statements about other matters.[13]

Tennessee's regulations on information that attorneys may disseminate about a case is described by the state supreme court in Disciplinary Rule 8 of the Code of Professional Responsibility.[14] Attorneys in state criminal proceedings are prohibited from publicly releasing information that might unduly influence the outcome of the trial or unfairly influence sentencing.[15] The state supreme court has held that the strictures against trial publicity imposed by such disciplinary rules do not violate an attorney's First Amendment rights.[16] The rule states that from the time of the first step in a criminal action until the beginning of the trial or disposition without trial, attorneys associated with the matter shall not give information relating to:

- the character, reputation, or prior criminal record of the accused;
- the possibility of a plea of guilty to the offense charged or to a lesser offense;

- the existence or contents of any confession, admission, or statement given by the accused or his refusal or failure to make a statement;
- the performance or results of any examinations or tests or the refusal or failure of the accused to submit to examinations or tests;
- the identity, testimony, or credibility of a prospective witness; and
- any opinion as the guilt or innocence of the accused, the evidence, or the merits of the case.

However, Rule 8 allows attorneys involved in the investigation of a criminal matter to state without elaboration:

- information contained in a public record;
- that the investigation is in progress;
- the general scope of the investigation including a description of the offense;
- a request for assistance in apprehending a suspect or in obtaining evidence;
- a warning to the public of any dangers;
- the name, age, residence, occupation, and family status of the accused;
- the identity of the victim of the crime;
- the fact, time, and place of arrest, resistance, pursuit, and use of weapons;
- the identity of investigating and arresting officers or agencies and the length of the investigation;
- at the time of seizure, a description of the physical evidence seized, other than a confession, admission, or statement;
- the nature, substance, or text of the charge;
- the scheduling or result of any step in the judicial proceedings; and
- that the accused denies the charges made against him.

In civil actions in Tennessee, lawyers and law firms are likewise prohibited by the Code of Professional Responsibility from making extrajudicial statements that are "reasonably likely" to interfere with a fair hearing or trial.[17]

Access to Judicial Proceedings

The public's right of access to judicial proceedings is not absolute. Pre-trial proceedings may be closed if the court finds that an open hearing would result in a "substantial probability"[18] of prejudice against the defendant. In criminal trials, the U.S. Supreme Court has observed that a courtroom may be closed if an "overriding interest" can overcome presumed openness.[19] However, the U.S. Supreme Court has held that access to criminal trials is implicit in the guarantees of the First Amendment[20] and that a First Amendment qualified right of access exists also for pre-trial criminal proceedings.[21]

The media are generally attentive to the news potential of pre-trial criminal proceedings for two main reasons: (1) most criminal cases do not reach trial; and (2) for those cases that do come to trial, decisions reached in the pre-trial criminal proceedings may significantly influence the outcome of the case.

It is at pre-trial that motions are made to reduce or dismiss the charges against the accused. Perhaps, a plea bargaining agreement is reached and presented to a judge. Other motions may involve requests to suppress evidence, to continue or postpone the case or to move the case to another jurisdiction. It is not uncommon that motions are made for a competency hearing for the accused and to quash subpoenas for witnesses or evidence. Also possible are challenges concerning jury selection, bail and judicial bias. The courts, however, mindful of the accused Sixth Amendment right to a "public trial by an impartial jury," are concerned about the potential impact news coverage of pre-trial proceedings could have on the defendant's rights.

The constitutionality of closing pre-trial hearings was first heard by the Supreme Court in 1979 when a newspaper challenged a pre-trial closing of a murder case on First and Sixth Amendment grounds.[22] The newspaper's First Amendment argument for access was rejected by the Court. In a 5 to 4 decision, the Court held that the Sixth Amendment's guarantee of a public trial was a personal right for the defendant. Although the Sixth Amendment assumes open trials as a norm, the Court majority said, the defendant could waive this right to a public trial.

One year later, in 1980, the Court ruled on the constitutionality of a First Amendment right of access to criminal trials. Noting that criminal trials historically have been open to the public and the media, the Court recognized that the public and the press have an implicit, but not absolute, First Amendment right to attend criminal trials. "Without the freedom to attend such [criminal] trials, which people have exercised for centuries, important aspects of freedom of speech and of the press could be eviscerated,"[23] the majority opinion said.

Noting in *Richmond* that the trial judge did not present findings in support of closure and that alternatives to closure existed that would ensure fairness to the defendant, the Court held that "absent an overriding interest articulated in findings, the trial of a criminal case must be open to the public."[24] The Court said the Sixth Amendment did not give the defendant a right to a private trial.

A footnote in the plurality opinion of *Richmond*, stated that the right of access could not be considered absolute. The fair administration of justice, said the Court, may require reasonable regulations to ensure such things as courtroom decorum or even preferential seating for media representatives.

The 6th Circuit Court of Appeals, the circuit that includes Tennessee, ruled in a 1987[25] case that it is the public to whom the First Amendment guarantees reasonable access to criminal proceedings and it is individuals, not the government, to whom First Amendment interests attach. To the extent that publicity is a disadvantage for the government, the court said, the government must tolerate it.

Following *Richmond* and rulings in other cases that found the closing of pre-trial hearings unjustified, the Court in 1986 applied a qualified First Amendment right of access to preliminary criminal hearings.[26] The Court considered access to pre-trial hearings to be no less essential than access to any other criminal justice process. It was the Court's judgment that preliminary hearings could be closed only if "(1) there is a substantial probability that the defendant's right to a fair trial will be prejudiced by publicity that the closure would prevent and (2) reasonable alternatives to closure cannot adequately protect the defendant's free trial rights."[27] In the 1986 *Press-Enterprise II* opinion, the Court also said grand jury proceedings required secrecy to function properly.

Local rules of the federal district court in Tennessee's Eastern District prohibit judges from restricting the media in the publication or broadcast of information the media has gathered about a criminal case.[28] The rules also provide that pre-trial criminal proceedings are open to the public unless on-the-record findings show that openness would "impair a defendant's right to a fair trial; and that reasonable alternatives to closure will not adequately protect the defendant's right to a fair trial."[29]

Rules governing access to criminal pre-trial proceedings and criminal trials in state courts were set by the Tennessee Supreme Court in 1985.[30] Drawing on the language of the U. S. Supreme Court's *Richmond* decision, the Tennessee court held, "The presumption of openness," the court said in *Drake*, "may be overcome only by an overriding interest based on findings that closure is essential to preserve higher values and is narrowly tailored to serve that interest."[31] Further, the court held that the overriding interest and findings must be "specific enough that a reviewing court can determine whether the closure order was properly entered."[32] It was the court's opinion in Drake that fair trial rights of a defendant and protection of sensitive information may in some instances require a closed trial, but such circumstances would be "rare, however, and the balance of interests must be struck with special care."[33]

The court also established in *Drake* certain rules that must be followed in seeking a closure order to a preliminary hearing. The closure request, usually by the defendant, must be in writing and state an "overriding interest that is likely to be prejudiced."[34] In granting the closure order, even if there have been no objections to the order, the trial judge must "consider reasonable alternatives to closing the proceedings, tailoring any closure order so that it is no broader than necessary to protect that interest." Those in opposition to a closure order have seven days to appeal the order before closure and a review of the appeal must be prompt.[35] Transcripts of closed criminal proceedings and trials are to be made public at the "earliest time consistent with the preservation of the interests that require the closure."[36]

Civil trials and proceedings traditionally are open to the public, but the law concerning the public's right of access is less clear in civil than criminal proceedings because the U.S. Supreme Court has yet to considered a First Amendment right of access to civil proceedings. However, the Court, in footnote 17 of the 1980 *Richmond* opinion, said both civil and criminal trials historically have been presumed open.[37]

As in criminal proceedings, lawyers in a civil proceeding are prohibited from giving information not on the public record if the information would interfere with a fair trial.[38] In a sensational civil or criminal trial, the federal court may further restrict lawyers from making certain statements[39] and may give special orders that relate to courtroom seating and conduct of the media and public, the sequestering of jurors and witnesses, and any other matter the court decides is necessary.[40]

What To Do If Faced With Closure

A Tennessee reporter has an opportunity to officially object to a closure motion even if absent from the courtroom at the time the motion for closure was made. This is possible because requests for closure must be made in writing and filed in the clerk's office at least three days before a hearing on the order is held.[41] The date and time of the hearing of the closure motion is set on the clerk's docket of cases. (Because no other notice of the hearing is required, however, a reporter should check the clerk's office daily for a closure hearing in a trial of interest.) Once aware of the closure request, a reporter should ask for a copy of the motion. A news organization should then file a written objection to the closure, along with a request for a hearing to present arguments against closure.

If present in the courtroom when closure is requested, a reporter should object immediately and ask to remain. In objecting, the reporter should be respectful of the judge, but ask to go on record against closure and ask for a recess so that counsel can be obtained to present arguments against closure. When going on the record, a reporter may say that the closure will violate state statutory and constitutional provision as demonstrated in the state supreme court decision in 1985, *Tennessee v. Drake*, and the decisions of the U.S. Supreme Court in *Press Enterprise I*, 1984, and *Press Enterprise II*, 1986. Then, the reporter should request a delay so that an attorney for the news organization can appear before the court to present legal arguments against closure.

If, after voicing an objection and going on the record, a reporter is asked to leave the courtroom, the reporter should comply because failure to comply could result in a contempt citation for failing to obey a court order and for disrupting the proceedings. It is inadvisable for a reporter to agree not to publish a report of the proceedings as a condition for remaining in a courtroom. If a reporter finds out what has occurred in a closed courtroom, a reporter may publish the information

Juvenile Proceedings and Records

In a 1982 case challenging the closure of a criminal trial because the sexual assault victim was a minor, the U. S. Supreme Court further clarified the boundaries of the First Amendment right of access. Justice William Brennan, writing for the majority, said that where "the state attempts to deny the right of access in order to inhibit the disclosure of sensitive information, it must be shown that the denial is necessitated by a compelling governmental interest and is narrowly tailored to serve that interest."[42] A state statute requiring a mandatory closing to protect juveniles in a criminal trial from harm was insufficient governmental interest, in the opinion of the Court.

Juvenile or paternity proceedings are quite another matter. In those circumstances, the Tennessee Rules of Juvenile Procedure allow proceedings to be closed to the media and the general public at the "discretion of the court."[43] Further, by statute,[44] hearings in juvenile courts may be closed to the public except where the purpose of the hearing is to declare a person in contempt of court or for juvenile traffic offenses. In addition, the judge may temporarily exclude the child from hearings except while allegations of his delinquency or unruly conduct are being heard.[45]

Except for traffic cases, files and records of juvenile courts are closed except to the following people: the judge, officers and professional staff of the court; parties to the proceeding and their counsel and representatives; a public or private agency or institution providing supervision or having custody of the child under order of the court; the court and its probation and other officials or professional staff and the attorney for the defendant for use in preparing a presentence report in a criminal case in which the defendant is convicted and who prior thereto had been a party to the proceeding in juvenile court.[46] In addition, the statute provides that the court may grant access to any other person, agency or institution with a legitimate interest in the proceeding or in the work of the court.

Law enforcement records involving juveniles in Tennessee are not open to the public unless the juvenile is tried as an adult, national security is involved, or the judge otherwise allows disclosure in the interest of the juvenile.[47]

If the media are allowed access to juvenile records and proceedings, information gained from those sources may be published or broadcasted.[48] In addition, the press may publish the name of a juvenile suspect whose name is lawfully gained, such as through routine monitoring of the police radio.[49]

Cameras and Recording Devices in Courtrooms

Cameras were banned for many years in courts after they played a role in notorious criminal cases that reached the U.S. Supreme Court.[50]

Two years after the highly publicized 1935 trial of Bruno Hauptmann for the kidnaping of the Charles Lindbergh baby, the American Bar Association in its Cannon of Professional Ethics adopted Cannon 35, which prohibited the taking of photographs in the courtroom even when the court was in recess.[51] When Canon 35 was updated, the restrictions were applied to broadcasting, televising and recording, except for ceremonial proceedings and the presentation of evidence.

While Canon 35 did not carry the force of law, it was widely adopted by judges. Then in 1965 a plurality of the Court in *Estes* expressed the view that televising the original trial prohibited the accused from a fair trial.[52] Following this opinion, cameras were effectively absent from courtrooms for many years.

Technological changes, including smaller, quieter cameras and faster film speeds that negated the need for special lighting, plus strong lobbying by media organizations and support from the bench brought about photographic coverage of some state court proceedings in the late 1970s. After the Supreme Court's ruling in 1981 in Chandler v. Florida, many more state courts began to set guidelines for broadcasting, televising and recording in the courtrooms.

In *Chandler*, the Court held that photographic coverage of criminal proceedings was not inherently prejudicial to defendants, even if the defendants objected to the coverage.[53] While the Court said that courtroom decorum must be maintained, the ruling allowed for states to adopt procedures for audio and video coverage of courtroom proceedings.

Federal Courtrooms

Photographic coverage of trials in federal courts is not permitted. However, from July 1991 until July 1994, on an experimental basis, the U. S. Judicial Conference is allowing coverage of civil proceedings in six federal district courts and two federal courts of appeals.[54] Presumably, the Judicial Conference will evaluate the three-year pilot program and consider opening more federal courtrooms to cameras.

A federal judge may authorize televising, recording, photographing or broadcasting ceremonial proceedings such as investiture and naturalization and for judicial, rather than media, purposes.[55] The rules for federal courts in the Eastern District of Tennessee, for example, prohibit the media from photographing, broadcasting, or recording in courtrooms or floors of the courthouse where district courts are conducted, without the approval of the case judge.[56]

Tennessee State Courts

State appellate and trial judges in Tennessee may authorize the broadcasting, televising and recording of proceedings. If allowed, the activity must be conducted under specific guidelines established by the Tennessee Supreme Court, must not detract from the proceedings, or interfere with a fair hearing.[57] In criminal trials the written consent of the accused must be obtained.

Witnesses, jurors, parties and attorneys must be notified that broadcasting, televising, or recording is planned and that each person has a right to object. If an objection to media coverage is made by a witness, juror, party or attorney prior to testimony, the judge will immediately stop the activity. Objections by an attorney or party will halt all photographic and electronic coverage. Objection by a witness or juror will prevent camera and audio coverage of only that person. A trial judge has the discretion to stop any media activity deemed prejudicial.[58]

Other rules governing media coverage of Tennessee state courts include:[59]

- No more than one television camera is permitted in the courtroom at any time while a hearing is in session, so if more than one news organization wants to broadcast, they must arrange for pool coverage.
- The media liaison must meet with the clerk of court or other person designated by the court in each court to determine placement of equipment for coverage of future proceedings.

- Wiring must be unobtrusive or hidden.
- Equipment cannot be installed or removed while court is in session.
- Overhead lights, when provided, must be switched on and off by the clerk or designee. No other lights, flashbulbs, flashes or sudden light changes may be used except with the express authorization of the clerk or designee of the court.
- No permanent installation shall be made nor shall any courtroom be altered unless approved in advance by the court. Any alterations to the courtroom for media coverage shall be paid for by the media.
- All television equipment is restricted to the area designated by the court.
- Television cameras must not produce distracting noise.
- The clerk or designee may allow wireless recording devices to be operated in the courtroom if they are not bulky, obtrusive, or noisy.
- The operator of wireless recording devices may sit at any place in the courtroom, but must not move from place to place except during the recess or between arguments.
- All recording devices must be carried upon the person of the operator and under no circumstances shall be left unattended in any location.
- Conferences between attorneys and their clients, between co-counsel of a client, between counsel and the presiding judge held at the bench, or of proceedings held in camera or when the jury is out must not be recorded or broadcast.

These guidelines do not preclude the coverage of a hearing by a news reporter or other person who is not using a camera or electronic equipment, but is taking notes or making sketches.

Neither do the restrictions apply to the coverage of investiture, ceremonial, or non-judicial proceedings.

Courts in several Tennessee counties have adopted additional rules concerning photographing, recording and broadcasting their proceedings. Local rules for circuit courts in Knox County, for example, provide that both the prosecution and defendant must give written consent before photographic or audio coverage will be allowed.

Local rules adopted in both Knox[60] and Hamilton[61] counties exclude video and audio coverage of any juror or potential juror. Hamilton County (Chattanooga) rules further specify that "no other television, camera, video, audio, electronic recording, and/or photographic equipment or devices will be permitted on the third floor (except within the confines of and accesses to, the District Attorney's office) at any time during any judicial proceeding. A trial judge may authorize specific exception for investiture or ceremonial events." Further, "interview of parties, attorneys, witnesses and other participants may not be conducted on the third floor. However, members of the media may contact such persons and request such interviews to be conducted elsewhere, provided that public use of passageways, halls, stairs, and elevators does not become impaired."[62]

Endnotes

1. Rule 21(a)(b) Tenn. R. Crim. Proc. provides: "In all criminal prosecutions the venue may be changed upon motion of the defendant, or upon the court's own motion with the consent of the defendant, if it appears to the court that, due to undue excitement against the defendant in the county where the offense was committed or any other cause, a fair trial probably could not be had. A motion for change of venue shall be accompanied by affidavit(s) averring facts constituting the alleged undue excitement or other cause upon which the motion is based. The State may file counter-affidavits."

2. See, for example, Eason v. State, 65 Tenn. 466 (1873); Conatser v. State, 80 Tenn. 436 (1883); Woods v. State, 99 Tenn. 182, 41 S.W. 811 (1897); Ward v. State, 102 Tenn. 724, 52 S.W. 996 (1899); Wilson v. State, 109 Tenn. 167, 70 S.W. 57 (1902); Turner v. State, 111 Tenn. 593, 69 S.W. 774 (1902); Palmer v. State, 121 Tenn. 465, 118 S.W. 1022 (1908).

3. Murphy v. Florida, 95 S.Ct. at 2036 (1975), quoting from Irvin v. Dowd, 81 S. Ct. 1639 (1961).

4. State v. Bates, 804 S.W.2d at 877. See also, State v. Sammons, 656 S.W.2d 869 (Tenn. Cr. App. 1982) and Manning v. State, 155 Tenn. 266, 292 S.W. 451, 455 (1927).

5. Rule 24(b)(2), Tenn. R. Crim. Proc.

6. State v. Sammons, 656 S.W.2d 869 (Tenn. Cr. App. 1982).

7. Adams, v. State, 563 S.W.2d at 806 (1978).

8. Id. at 807.

9. Clariday v. State, 552 S.W.2d 759 (1976).

10. Nebraska Press Association v. Stuart, 427 U.S. 539, 96 S.Ct. 2791 (1976).

11. Local Rules, U.S. Dist. Ct. E.D. Tenn., 83.2(b), Public Statements by Attorneys Concerning Criminal Proceedings, 1991.

12. Id.

13. Local Rules, U.S.. Dist. Ct. E.D. Tenn., 83.2(a), Public Statements by Attorneys Concerning Civil Proceedings, 1991.

14. Tenn. Rules of the S.Ctr., Rule 8, Code of Professional Responsibility, DR 7-107.

15. Id..

16. Zimmerman v. Board of Professional Responsibility, 764 S.W.2d 757 (Tenn. 1989), cert. denied, 109 S.Ct. 3160 (1989).

17. Id.

18. Press-Enterprise Co. v. Superior Court (II), 478 U.S. 1, 106 S.Ct. 2735, 92 L.Ed.2d 1, 13 Med. L. Rptr. 1001 (1986)

19. Richmond Newspapers, Inc. v. Virginia, 448 U.S. 555, 100 S. Ct. 2814, 65 L.Ed.2d 973, 6 Med. L. Rptr. 1833 (1980).

20. Id..

21. Press-Enterprise Co. v. Superior Court (II), 478 U.S. 1, 106 S.Ct. 2735, 92 L.Ed.2d 1, 13 Med. L. Rptr. 1001 (1986).

22. Gannett Co., Inc. v. De Pasquale, 443 U.S. 368, 99 S.Ct. 2898.

23. Richmond Newspapers, Inc. v. Virginia, 448 U.S. 555, 100 S. Ct. 2814, 65 L.Ed.2d 973, 6 Med. L. Rptr. 1833 (1980).

24. Id..

25. U. S. v. Ford, 830 F.2d 596.

26. Press-Enterprise Co. v. Superior Court (II), 478 U.S. 1, 106 S.Ct.2735, 92 L.Ed.2d 1, 13 Med. L. Rptr. 1001.

27. Id..

28. Local Rules, U.S. Dist. Ct. E.D. Tenn., 83.2(d), Provisions for Ensuring the Right to Open Trials and a Free Press, 1991.

29. Id.

30. Tennessee v. Drake, 701 S.W.2d 604, 12 Med. L. Rptr. 1488 (1985).

31. Id. at 607.

32. Id.

33. Id.

34. Id. at 608.

35. Id.

36. Id.

37. Richmond Newspapers, Inc. v. Virginia, 448 U.S. 555, 100 S. Ct. 2814, 65 L.Ed.2d 973, 6 Med. L. Rptr. 1833 (1980).

38. Local Rules, U.S.. Dist. Ct. E.D. Tenn., 83.2(a), Public Statements by Attorneys Concerning Civil Proceedings, 1991; Tenn. S. Ct., Rule 8, Code of Professional Responsibility, DR 7-107.

39. Local Rules, U.S. Dist. Ct. E.D. Tenn., 83.2(c), Provisions for Special Orders in Widely Publicized or Sensational Civil and Criminal Cases, 1991.

40. Id.

41. Tennessee v. Drake, 701 S.W.2d 604, 12 Med. L. Rptr. 1488.

42. Globe Newspaper Co. v. Superior Court, 102 S.Ct. 2613 (1982).

43. Tenn. Rules of the S. Ctr., Rules of Juvenile Procedure, Rule 27.

44. T.C.A. 37-1-124(d).

45. Id.

46. T.C.A. 37-1-153.

47. T.C.A. 37-1-154.

48. OAG 81-268; Cox Broadcasting Corp. v. Cohn, 420 U.S. 469, 95 S.Ct., 1029, 43 L.Ed.2d 328 (1975).

49. Smith v. Daily Mail Pub. Co., 443 U.S. 97 (1979).

50. Estes v. Texas, 381 U.S. 532, 85 S.Ct. 1628 (1965); Sheppard v. Maxwell, 384 U.S. 33, 86 S. Ct. 1507 (1966).

51. Canon 35 was updated by the American Bar Association's Canon of Judicial Conduct 3(7).

52. Estes v. Texas, 381 U.S. 532, 85 S.Ct. 1628 (1965).

53. Chandler v. Florida, 449 U.S. 560, 101 S. Ct. 802 (1981).

54. In re Judicial Conference Guidelines, 18 Med. L. Rptr. 1270 (1990); Fatzer, H., "Federal Courts Begin Experiment with Cameras," The Media and the Law, (Summer, 1991), 18-19.

55. In re Judicial Conference Guidelines, 18 Med. L. Rptr. 1270 (1990).

56. Local Rules, U.S.. Dist. Ct. E.D. Tenn.,83.2(f), Television and Radio Broadcasting, Tape Recording or Photographing Judicial Proceedings, 1991.

57. Tenn. S.Ct., Rule 10, Code of Judicial Conduct, Canon 3.

58. Id.

59. Id.

60. Knox County Local Rules of Practice. Rules of Practice of the Circuit Court for Knox County, Divisions I, II and III, Additional Rule (adopted October 29, 1979).

61. Hamilton County Local Rules of Practice, Local Rules of Practice in the Criminal Court Hamilton County, Rule 15 (effective March 2, 1990).

62. *Id.*

Access to Places

While the U.S.Supreme Court has recognized a First Amendment right to gather news,[1] the media's rights generally extend no further than those of the general public. Courts have rejected arguments that access to information is essential to the news gathering function and that because the press serves as a surrogate for the public, it should be granted access in circumstances where attendance must be limited. In some situations, on a voluntary basis rather than as a constitutional mandate, the press has been given special access and space considerations not afforded the general public. Examples are press facilities in the White House and both bodies of Congress and special seating for members of the media in some courtrooms and publicly owned auditoriums and sports arenas.

Access to Public Property

Public Forum Sites

Journalists, like the public at large, have access to publicly owned property that is considered a public forum, such as sidewalks and parks. Even here, however, the First Amendment is not an absolute. Government may regulate access to and use of public forum property under the following conditions:[2]

- the regulation directly relates to a valid governmental interest;
- the regulation is no broader than necessary to accomplish the valid interest;
- the regulation is based on non-content considerations, such as time, place and manner;
- alternative channels of communication exist.

Further, guidelines for administering the regulations must be clearly established so as discretionary authority on the part of public officials is eliminated. Using these or similar criteria, courts have struck down as unconstitutional laws that prohibited the door-to-door distribution of religious literature,[3] gave officials discretionary power to issue or deny permits for newspaper vending boxes,[4] subjected door-to-door commercial solicitors to greater restrictions than solicitors for religious, charitable, or political purposes,[5] or granted parade permits on a discriminatory basis.[6]

The Tennessee Supreme Court invalidated a section of an ordinance that prohibited throwing, depositing, or distributing commercial or noncommercial handbills, except for ideological matter, in or on any private premises.[7] The court reasoned that the section violated both the U.S. Constitution and Article I, Section 19 of the Tennessee Constitution because it was neither content neutral nor least restrictive.

Non Public Forum

The First Amendment does not protect access to publicly owned property that traditionally has not been open as a public forum—classrooms of public schools, public office buildings or prison facilities, for example. Demonstrations or newsgathering can be "reasonably,"[8] restricted in those areas on the basis that such activities would interfere with normal operations.

Access to airports: In a June 1992 decision, the U. S. Supreme Court held that airports, whether publicly or privately owned, are not public forums. In a 5-4 decision, the majority noted that the need for security leads to greater restrictions on public access to airports than on other forms of public transportation and that airports are not built for the purpose of providing a forum for expression. Thus, the majority concluded that a regulation barring solicitation of money at airports was a reasonable restriction to prevent fraud and pedestrian congestion.[9]

On the other hand, the court held that a ban on selling and distributing leaflets was not reasonable because it would "close the marketplace of ideas to less affluent organizations and speakers, leaving speech as the preserve of those who are able to fund themselves."[10]

Access to prisons and inmates: Reasoning that the media have no right of access greater than that afforded the general public, courts have denied journalists' attempts to go into non-public areas of prisons[11] or to interview specific inmates.[12] The

High Court acknowledged the importance of the press in providing the public with information about jail conditions, but, on balance, the Court has given greater weight to prison officials' concerns about prison security, inmate privacy, and allowing some prisoners a forum that would give them a disproportionate degree of notoriety and influence among their fellow inmates. State and federal courts have used the U.S. Supreme Court's holdings in prison access cases to deny broadcasters' requests to televise executions.[13]

Where access to specific inmates has been denied, journalists have sometimes been able to gain interviews by contacting the inmate's attorney and arranging to be put on the visitor's list.

The Tennessee Department of Correction has established procedures and guidelines for contacts between the media and TDOC officials and inmates.[14] Media representatives are permitted access to institutions, field offices, and community-based programs, provided that the warden, director or designee agrees to grant access. Interviews or visits may be denied, suspended, or terminated when a contingency plan has been implemented or "under any other circumstances that pose a threat to the continued safety or persons and/or the security of the facility or office." If access is denied, procedures require that the prison official making the decision provide a written explanation to the TDOC regional administrator, assistant commissioner and information officer.[15] The guidelines state that offenders' right to privacy shall be preserved and that media representatives "shall be made aware of their responsibilities regarding privacy, custody, and security."[16]

In Tennessee, personal interviews with incarcerated offenders are subject to, but not limited to, the following restrictions:[17]

- Interviews are voluntary. Before meeting a media representative, an offender must sign a release, which becomes part of the offender's official file. The release form indicates the subject matter of the interview and specifically notes that anything said during an interview may be used against the offender in a court of law at any time.
- Hours for interviews are 8 a.m. to 4:30 p.m. Monday through Friday, except for holidays.

- All interviews shall be conducted in person and one-on-one. Offenders are not allowed to talk with more than one media representative at the same time.
- The warden will select the location for the interview.
- Live broadcasts via television, radio, telephone or other electronic or communicative method from inside the perimeter of a TDOC institution are not permitted at any time.
- Offenders may not participate in a live broadcast program unless directly authorized by the TDOC commissioner.
- Interviews must take place on institutional grounds unless directly authorized by the TDOC commissioner.

Personal interviews with TDOC staff members are subject to the following restrictions:[18]

- The staff member must obtain prior approval from the facility administrator for any interview conducted during the employee's working hours or state property.
- Interviews are voluntary.
- Requests by the media for a staff member's home address or telephone number must be made in writing. A copy of the request shall be placed in the employee's file[19] and a copy forwarded to the employee's home address and to the information officer at the institution.

The information officer, warden, director, or designee are authorized to release to the media the following information about an offender: name, age, race, conviction and sentencing data, general institutional assignments.[20] They are also authorized to make an identification picture available for copying.[21]

Public property leased to private parties: Questions have arisen about access to public buildings that have been leased to a private organizations for a newsworthy event. Does the private entity have the authority to grant exclusive coverage of the event to a single television network?

Courts are divided on whether this constitutes state action, which, under equal protection and due process laws, requires the existence of rational, nonarbitrary guidelines to determine who should have access. For example, a federal district court in Hartford, Conn., held that the city was acting in a proprietary manner when it rented its civic auditorium to a private organization for a national figure skating championships.[22] The organization granted exclusive television rights to ABC. Under this court's ruling, other television networks had no recourse.

On the other hand, a court in Cleveland, Ohio, held that state action was involved when a private group leased a publicly owned civic center.[23] Thus, the organization could not discriminate in allowing some newsgatherers to attend while barring others.

In a case involving municipally owned Yankee Stadium in New York City, a court held that it was a violation of due process and equal protection rights to bar female reporters from locker rooms because a less restrictive alternative to total exclusion could be used to protect athletes' privacy.[24]

Discriminatory access: On the grounds that they did not promote a compelling state interest or were not the least restrictive means available to achieve the asserted purpose, courts have struck down policies that required reporters for a particular newspaper to submit all questions in writing[25] and to make an appointment to obtain information.[26] Competing media in each case did not have to conform to the restrictive policies.

Where the press is provided special facilities on a voluntary basis—such as the White House press room—access must not be denied on a discriminatory basis to journalists who meet specified requirements. Where the Secret Service refused to grant a White House press pass to a reporter who had credentials for the House and Senate press galleries, a court said the Secret Service must make known the specific guidelines for granting press passes. It was too general to say that the reporter in question was being denied access because of "reasons of security."[27]

Access to Scenes of Crises

Journalists have no guaranteed right of access to accident or disaster sites or scenes of other newsworthy events on either private or public property. The Supreme Court has observed that "newsgathering is not without its First Amendment protections,"[28] but that protection may have to yield to competing interests. Reasonable restrictions are allowed on press access and movement at crises scenes, and journalists who disobey police orders may be arrested for disorderly conduct or criminal trespass or may be held liable in a civil action.

Tennessee's statute on disorderly conduct makes it a criminal offense for anyone in a public place and with intent to cause public annoyance or alarm to refuse "to obey an official order to disperse issued to maintain public safety in dangerous proximity to a fire, hazard or other emergency."[29] The statute has not been used in the context of newsgathering activities.

In upholding the disorderly conduct conviction of a photographer who disobeyed a police order to leave the scene of a fatal car accident, a New Jersey court held that "whether a newsperson's conduct is disorderly must turn on whether, from an objective standpoint and under all of the circumstances, the policeman's order to the newsman was reasonable, taking into account the special role performed by the press."[30]

The Wisconsin Supreme Court ruled similarly in upholding the disorderly conduct conviction of a television cameraman who repeatedly refused to leave the scene of a airliner crash in a non-public area of a publicly owned airport. The court said officers on the scene "must be accorded discretion to regulate conduct therein" so long as the regulation is "reasonably designed to preserve good order."[31]

In another case reporters were found guilty of criminal trespass after they accompanied demonstrators onto the grounds of a nuclear power plant construction site instead of remaining in the viewing area provided for the press.[32] The Oklahoma court ruled that the First Amendment right of access to newsworthy events is outweighed by legitimate state interests in protecting property rights and in maintaining law and order.

Access to Polling Places

Several states in recent years have passed laws prohibiting the media from conducting "exit interviews" or public opinion polls near polling sites. The legislative concern–particularly in Western states–is that potential voters will not bother to cast ballots if the media have already projected the outcome of a national election, based on exit interviews with voters in other time zones. Thus, the outcomes of state and local elections will determined by fewer voters.

State statutes in Washington,[33] Minnesota,[34] Florida,[35] and Montana[36] that prohibited exit polls or public opinion polls within a specified distance of a polling place have been held unconstitutional. A 250-foot exclusion in Georgia was also held unconstitutional, until the judge decided that the statute could be interpreted to limit the prohibition to 25 feet, which would pass constitutional muster.[37]

The Tennessee General Assembly has not enacted a statute regulating exit interviews, but the legislature has banned campaign literature or the solicitation of votes within 100 feet of a polling place. This Tennessee law was upheld by the U.S. Supreme Court in 1992.[38] The court held that by attempting to balance the conflict between two fundamental–rights the exercise of free speech and right to vote without intimidation or fraud– the state's compromise with the 100-foot campaign-free zone was sufficiently narrow to be constitutional.

Access to Private Property

Neither the U.S. Supreme Court nor the Tennessee Supreme Court have specifically considered whether the media have a legal right to enter private property in pursuit of news.

[For examples of cases where journalists in pursuit of stories were subsequently sued in tort actions, see the section titled "Newsgathering on Private Property" in the Privacy chapter in this book.]

Endnotes

1. Richmond Newspapers Inc. v. Va., 448 U.S. 555 (1980).
2. See, e.g., Freeman v. Burson, 802 S.W.2d 210 (Tenn 1990).
3. Martin v. Struthers, 319 U.S. 141 (1943).
4. City of Lakewood v. Plain Dealer Pub. Co., 486 U.S. 750 (1988).
5. Chicago Tribune Co. v. Village of Downers Grove, 1245 Ill.2d 468, 532 N.E.2d 821 (1988).
6. Village of Skokie v. National Socialist Party of America, 69 Ill.2d 605, 373 N.E.2d 21 (1978).
7. H & L Messengers, Inc. v. City of Brentwood, 577 S.W.2d 444 (Tenn. 1979).
8. International Society for Krishna Consciousness Inc. v. Lee, 112 S.Ct. 2701 (1992).
9. Id.
10. Id., Justice Anthony Kennedy concurring.

11. Houchins v. KQED, 438 U.S. 1 (1978).

12. Pell v. Procunier, 417 U.S. 817 (1974); Saxbe v. Washington Post Co., 417 U.S. 843 (1974).

13. Garrett v. Estelle, 556 F.2d 1274, 2 Media Law Rptr. 2265 (5th Cir. 1977), cert. denied 438 U.S. 914 (1978). Kearns-Tribune v. Utah Board of Corrections, 2 Media Law Rptr. 1353 (DC Utah 1977).

14. Tennessee Department of Correction Administrative Policies and Procedures, No. 103.04.

15. Id. (VI)(A)(1)(3).

16. Id.(VI)(A)(2).

17. Id.(B).

18. Id. (C).

19. Employee records are open to public inspection under T.C.A. 10-7-503.

20. Tennessee Department of Correction Administrative Policies and Procedures, No. 103.04(D).

21. Id.(D)(6).

22. Post-Newsweek Stations Inc. v. Traveler's Insurance Co., 518 F.Supp. 81 (D.Conn. 1981); see also D'Amario v. Providence Civic Center Authority, 783 F.2d 1 (1st Cir.) (reversed and remanded), 639 F.Supp. 1538 (D.R.I. 1986) (complaint dismissed).

23. NBC v. Association of State Democratic Chairs, 14 Media Law Rept. 1383 (N.D. Ohio 1987).

24. Ludtke v. Kuhn, 461 F.Supp. 86 (S.D. N.Y. 1978).

25. Times-Picayune Pub. Corp. v. Lee, 15 Media Law Rept. 1713 (E.D. La. 1988) (unpublished case).

26. Southwestern Newspapers Corp. v. Curtis, 584 S.W.2d 362, 5 Media Law Rptr. 1914 (Tex. Civ. App. 1979).

27. Sherrill v. Knight, 569 F.2d 124, 3 Media Law Rept. 1514 (D.C. Cir. 1977).

28. Branzburg v. Hayes, 408 U.S. 665 (1972).

29. T.C.A. 39-17-305 (a)(2).

30. New Jersey v. Lashinsky, 404 A.2d 1121 (N.J. 1979).

31. City of Oak Creek v. Ah King, 436 N.W.2d 285 (1989).

32. Oklahoma v. Bernstein, 5 Media Law Rptr. 2313 (1980, affirmed Stahl v. State, 665 P.2d 839, 9 Media Law Rptr. 1945 (Okla. Crim. 1983), cert. denied, 464 U.S. 1069 (1984).

33. Daily Herald v. Munro, 838 F.2d 380, 14 Media Law Rptr. 2333 (9th Cir. 1987).

34. CBS Inc. v. Growe, 15 Media Law Rept. 2275 (D. Minn. 1988).

35. CBS Inc., et. al. v. Smith, 681 F.Supp. 794 (S.D. Fla. 1988).

36. National Broadcasting Co. v. Colburg, 699 F. Supp. 241 (D. Mont. 1988). See also Journal Broadcasting of Kentucky v. Logsdon, No. C88-0147-L(A) (W.D. Ky. 1988), NBC v. Karpan, No. C88-0320-B (D. Wyo. 1988), Charleston Television Inc. v. Charleston County Election Commission, No. 88-CP-10-4860 (S.C. Sup. Ct. 1988).

37. NBC v. Cleland, 697 F.Supp. 1204 (N.D.Ga. 1988).
38. Burson v. Freeman, 1992 WL 107344, 20 Media Law Rptr. 1137.

Contempt of Court, Compelled Disclosure and Search Warrants

Contempt of court problems involving journalists generally come under one of two circumstances: where a judge considers published material an interference with the administration of justice or where journalists refuse to comply with a subpoena to give testimony about information from confidential sources or to supply out-takes or other unpublished material.

Contempt of Court

As a means of insuring respect for their authority and compliance with their orders, judges may exercise summary contempt power,[1] meaning that the judge has the authority to find the offender guilty and pass sentence without a hearing.[2] In Tennessee, courts also have a statutory right "to issue attachments and inflict punishments for contempts of court" in the following situations:[3]

- The willful misbehavior of any person in the presence of the court, or so near thereto as to obstruct the administration of justice.
- The willful misbehavior of court officers in their official transactions.
- The willful disobedience or resistance of any court officer, party, juror, witness, or any other person, to any lawful writ, process, order, rule, decree, or court command.
- Abuse of, or unlawful interference with, the process or proceedings of the court.
- Willfully conversing with jurors in relation to the merits of the cause in the trial of which they are engaged, or otherwise tampering with them.
- Any other act or omission declared a contempt by law.

Classifications of Contempt

Both civil and criminal contempt are recognized by Tennessee courts with the distinction resting on the purpose of the punishment. Civil contempt is used to compel compliance with court orders, whereas criminal contempt is meant to punish one who interferes with the orderly administration of justice by some act, such as attacking the dignity and authority of the court.

For example, if a person who has been found liable for damages in a lawsuit refuses to pay, the person owed the money may petition the court to hold him or her in civil contempt until the damages have been paid. It has been said that the offender in a civil contempt possesses the keys to the jail cell because compliance with the court order will bring release. In criminal contempt, the damage has been done and cannot be undone; thus, the contempt citation is meant to punish and to deter repetitions of the offending act.

Contempt is further classified as "direct" and "indirect" contempt. Direct contempt refers to a contemptuous act that occurs in the presence of the judge or so near thereto that it interferes with court proceedings.[4] For example, taking a photograph in a courtroom or near the courtroom where such photographing was not allowed would be direct contempt.

Indirect contempt is based upon acts not committed in the presence of the court, but which a judge thinks interferes with the administration of justice. Indirect contempt may be punished only after the offender has been given notice, and the opportunity to respond to the charges at a hearing.[5] An example of indirect contempt would be to publish information in violation of a restrictive order.

Contempt for Publishing Information

In an 1868 case,[6] the Tennessee Supreme Court held that courts have the power to prevent the publication of testimony and other proceedings, during the progress of the trial of a case. The court also held that courts have the inherent right and power to punish newspaper publishers for contempt who, pending the trial of a case, publish material that is calculated to impede, embarrass, or affect the orderly trial and disposition of the case being heard.[7] The contempt power for publishing material that hinders or embarrasses the court during pending litigation does not depend upon any preliminary order forbidding such publication.[8]

The state supreme court has ruled further that contempt power and the mode of preventing the publication rest largely in the discretion of the judge and that it is, in its nature and the occasion and manner of its exercise, without the possibility of control by a supervising court.[9] This grant of discretionary power to judges concerning a pending trial has never been expressly overturned by Tennessee courts, but it could not withstand constitutional scrutiny today in light of more recent U.S. Supreme Court decisions. In three cases during the 1940s, the High Court limited the power of judges to punish out-of-court publications to those that constituted a "clear and present danger to the administration of justice."[10]

The earliest Tennessee contempt cases,[11] as applied to published newspaper articles about trials, emphasized that a trial was pending at the time the articles were published. In a later case,[12] a publisher was held in contempt after his newspaper named a circuit court judge, described him as being wholly unfit and incapacitated to hold court, and said that the court had broken down and ceased to function. On appeal, the citation was held invalid because the published material did not relate to a pending suit, nor did it question the integrity of the court. The state supreme court held that the pertinent part of the statute[13] granting contempt power to judges relates to direct personal misbehavior and could not be extended so as to embrace the effect that a newspaper article, published at some remote place, might have upon those who happened to read it.[14]

The U.S. Supreme Court has taken the position that judges should be "thick-skinned" and able to take criticism about their official actions.[15] Rather than holding the publisher of a critical article in contempt, a judge, of course, has the right, like other citizens, to pursue a civil libel suit and to attempt to meet the required burdens of proof for false, defamatory statements made with reckless disregard for truth.

The Tennessee Shield Law

In addition to out-of-court publications about pending cases, journalists have been cited for contempt in situations where they refused to comply with subpoenas seeking unpublished material or the identity of confidential sources. While both state and federal courts have recognized a legal exemption from compelled testimony to persons in certain relationships—husband-wife, priest-penitent, attorney-client, doctor-patient—no such privileged relationship has been recognized in common law for journalists and their sources.

In three cases that were joined at the U.S. Supreme Court in 1972,[16] the news media argued for a constitutional right against compelled disclosure, reasoning that reliance on confidential sources was often essential to news gathering, which was protected by the First Amendment. A sharply divided Supreme Court voted against recognition of a constitutional privilege for journalists or other information gathers. Four justices favored recognition; four did not, and Justice Lewis Powell, who voted with the majority against the privilege, favored it in some circumstances. Powell advocated an approach in which, on a case by case basis, freedom of the press would be balanced against the obligation of all citizens to give relevant testimony with respect to criminal conduct. In a dissenting opinion, Justice Potter Stewart set forth a three-part test that the government or other party seeking confidential information should meet before requiring journalists to testify.

Justice Stewart's three-part test became the basis of a conditional privilege granted nine months later by the Tennessee legislature. The state shield law[17] protects a person "engaged in gathering information for publication or broadcast connected with or employed by the news media or press, or who is independently engaged in gathering information for publication or broadcast" from being required by "a court, a grand jury, the legislature, or any administrative body, to disclose before the general assembly or any Tennessee court, grand jury, agency, department, or commission any information or the source of any information procured for publication or broadcast."[18]

The statute specifies these conditions under which a court might order this protection divested:

- "There is probable cause to believe that the person from whom the information is sought has information which is clearly relevant to a specific probable violation of law;[19]
- "The person has demonstrated that the information sought cannot reasonably be obtained by alternative means; and[20]

- "The person has demonstrated a compelling and overriding public interest of the people of the state of Tennessee in the information."[21]

The burden of meeting the three-part test by "clear and convincing evidence" is on the party seeking the information.[22] The privilege does not shield sources of allegedly defamatory information in cases where defendants in a civil action for defamation assert a defense based on the source of such information.[23] The statute also provides that a judgment divesting the protection shall be stayed, pending an expedited appeal to the court of appeals.[24] Furthermore, the court of appeals "shall make an independent determination . . . to the facts in the record and shall not accord a presumption of correctness to the trial court's findings."[25]

During the twenty years since the Tennessee shield law was enacted, appellate courts in the state had several occasions to interpret the statute as it applies to news media.[26] Legal principles growing out of those cases indicate that the statute applies to both civil and criminal cases, as well as to both confidential and nonconfidential information.[27] This means that journalists seeking protection under the shield law do not have to establish that a confidential relationship existed between them and their sources. The principle is also important to protect out-takes, notes, or other unpublished material collected under nonconfidential circumstances.

In 1987, the Tennessee Supreme Court ruled that a radio reporter should not be divested of the privilege because the state had not demonstrated by clear and convincing evidence that the police had investigated the situation and that no alternative sources were available.[28] In that case a broadcaster who had aired an interview in which an unidentified man confessed to a murder was subpoenaed to appear before a grand jury. An audio tape and transcript of the broadcast were insufficient evidence, the court held, to deny the broadcaster protection under the statute. A subpoena to compel testimony was quashed in a 1991 case when the Tennessee court of appeals held that the subpoenaed reporter had no relevant information that could not be obtained by alternative means. In that case two city officials admitted statements attributed to them in a newspaper article about the dismissal of a chief of police.[29]

The state qualified shield law may not protect Tennessee journalists who are subpoenaed in a lawsuit raising issues under the federal Constitution or a federal statute. Under such circumstances, a news organization may argue that the Constitution provides a conditional privilege. After the 1972 Branzburg decision at the U.S. Supreme Court, many courts have read the dissenting and concurring opinions as creating a federal constitutional privilege.[30]

Suggestions for Handling a Subpoena

In consultation with news organization management and attorneys, journalists served with a subpoena generally take one of three approaches: move to quash the subpoena, appear as directed by the subpoena but assert privilege as each question is asked, or comply with the subpoena.

The following guidelines have been suggested by news organizations and professional associations:

- Do not accept service of a subpoena over the telephone. Tennessee law does not require personal service if the person being served agrees to accept service via telephone.
- Do not accept a subpoena for someone else or allow anyone to accept one for you.
- Do not accept an unsigned subpoena or one without all the blanks completed. Tennessee law specifies that a subpoena must be signed by the clerk or other authorized officer of the court.[31]
- At the time the subpoena is served, do not answer any questions or offer any information to the subpoena server.
- Do not agree to the subpoena server that you will appear voluntarily.
- After receiving a subpoena, make a detailed, accurate record of how, when, and by whom you were served.
- Do not destroy any materials requested by the subpoena. This is illegal.
- Immediately report the receipt of a subpoena to your immediate supervising editor. An attorney for your news organization will probably want to contact the attorney representing

the subpoenaing party to learn the nature of the proceeding and testimony sought.

- Follow the instructions of your supervising editor or attorney. Do not contact or talk with subpoenaing parties or attorneys because you may inadvertently waive some of your rights.
- Do not agree in advance of your scheduled appearance to allow anyone to examine materials sought.
- If unpublished material or transcripts are requested, have your attorney petition the court to quash the subpoena. Even if the petition to quash is denied, this process will allow you and your attorneys more time to organize your opposition. Too, circumstances may change. The grand jury term may end or the investigation may be dropped for some other reason.
- Seek appropriate payment for the reasonable costs of producing materials requested.

Violating Promises of Confidentiality

Does liability exist for a news organization that reveals a source's name after promising to keep his identity secret? This question was answered in the affirmative by the U.S. Supreme Court in a 1991 case.[32] Several newspaper and broadcast reporters in Minneapolis promised political consultant Dan Cohen confidentiality in exchange for some damaging information about a political candidate. Editors at the newspapers, against their reporters' wishes, decided that Cohen's use of last-minute dirty politics was no less newsworthy than the damaging information he disclosed, so his name was used in the story.

Cohen sued the Minneapolis newspapers, alleging that he had been damaged by fraudulent misrepresentation and breach of contract. The Supreme Court held that the news organization was not protected by the Constitution in this situation because the promise of confidentiality amounted to an oral contract, enforceable as such.

Search Warrants

News organizations have dealt with newsroom searches less frequently than with subpoenas, and few court cases exist in this area. Law enforcement officials have sometimes conducted a newsroom search after failing to gain desired information through the subpoena process or when immediacy precludes using the subpoena process. The media have argued unsuccessfully that such searches are seriously disruptive of the reporting process and in violation of constitutional free expression guarantees.[33] In response to the U.S. Supreme Court's refusal of that argument, Congress enacted the Privacy Protection Act of 1980.[34] The statute prohibits officials—both state and federal—from searching for or seizing documentary materials or work product materials "possessed by a person reasonably believed to have a purpose to disseminate to the public a newspaper, book, broadcast, or other similar form of public communication."

As defined by the statute, "documentary materials" and "work product materials" do not include "contraband or the fruits of a crime or things otherwise criminally possessed, or property designed or intended for use, or which is or has been used as, the means of committing a criminal offense." Further, the statute exempts these circumstances:

- There is probable cause to believe that the person possessing the materials has committed or is committing the crime to which the materials relate;
- There is reason to believe that seizure is necessary to prevent death or serious bodily injury;
- There is reason to believe that giving notice pursuant to a subpoena *duces tecum* would result in the destruction, alteration, or concealment of such materials; or
- The materials have not been produced in response to a court order and all appellate remedies have been exhausted, or there is reason to believe delay in an investigation or a trial resulting from further proceedings would threaten the interests of justice.

The act permits a civil cause of action for damages and entitles the victim of an illegal search to recover actual damages, attorney's fees and court costs.

Suggestions for Handling a Newsroom Search

Before facing law enforcement officials armed with search warrants, news organizations may want to consider the following suggestions:

- Establish internal procedures to ensure that top management and legal counsel are notified immediately when a search warrant is served.
- The top-ranking management person in the newsroom at the time should ask that the search be delayed until an attorney arrives to represent the news organization.
- If the request for delay is denied, other delaying tactics may be used to provide more time for an attorney to arrive. The editor in charge should read the warrant carefully to ensure that it specifically identifies the property to be searched and seized.
- Remain polite to the officials.
- Request that the number of officers conducting the search be limited to a reasonable number so as to be less disruptive of on-going newsroom operations.
- Never indicate that you consent or otherwise agree to the search.
- Do not interfere with the search once it begins, but try to deter the zeal of searchers by asking for and recording the name of each person involved and badge number of police officers.
- Advise the searchers that they may be liable for actual damages, attorney's fees and court costs under the Privacy Protection Act of 1980 unless one of the exceptions permitted under that law applies in this particular search.
- You need not answer any questions or give the searchers any material; however, it may be advantageous to give them material specified in the warrant rather than letting them go through files where other sensitive documents may be uncovered.
- An editor or other management personnel should accompany the searchers at all times.
- Record the search on film or tape, making sure that at least one picture is taken of each person involved.

- **Demand a formal inventory of each document or object seized or examined during the search. An editor or staff member should make a similar inventory as the search proceeds.**
- **After the search, if you think the Privacy Protection Act of 1980 has been violated, file a civil suit for damages.**

Endnotes

1. 18 U.S.C.A. 401.

2. For a sentence of six months imprisonment or greater, a jury trial is required unless waived. Bloom v. State of Illinois, 391 U.S. 216 (1968).

3. T.C.A. 29-9-102.

4. State v. Maddux, 571 S.W.2d 819 (Tenn. 1978).

5. Id.

6. State v. Galloway, 45 Tenn. 326, 98 Am. Dec. 404.

7. Tate v. State ex rel. Raine, 132 Tenn. 131, 177 S.W. 69 (1915).

8. Id.

9. Id.

10. Bridges v. California, 314 U.S. 252 (1941); Pennekamp v. Florida, 328 U.S. 331 (1946); Craig v. Harney, 331 U.S. 367 (1947).

11. Tate v. State ex rel. Raine, 132 Tenn. 131, 177 S.W. 69 (1915) and State v. Galloway, 45 Tenn. 326 (1868).

12. In re Hickey, 149 Tenn. 344, 258 S.W. 417 (1923).

13. T.C.A. 29-9-102 Subdivision (1).

14. In re Hickey, 149 Tenn. 344, 258 S.W. 417 (1923).

15. Bridges v. California, 314 U.S. 252 (1941).

16. Branzburg v. Hayes, 408 U.S. 665.

17. T.C.A. 24-1-208.

18. Id.(a).

19. Id. (2)(A).

20. Id. (2)(B).

21. Id. (2)(C).

22. Id. (2).

23. Id. (b).

24. Id. (B).

25. Id.(C).

26. See, e.g., Austin v. Memphis Publishing Co. 655 S.W.2d 146 (Tenn. 1983); State ex rel. Gerbitz v. Curriden, 738 S.W.2d 192 (Tenn. 1987); Dingman v. Harvel, 814 S.W.2d 362 (Tenn. App. 1991) (appeal denied).

27. Austin v. Memphis Publishing Co. 655 S.W.2d 146 (Tenn. 1983).

28. State ex rel. Gerbitz v. Curriden, 738 S.W.2d 192 (Tenn. 1987).

29. Dingman v. Harvel, 814 S.W.2d 362 (Tenn. App. 1991) (appeal denied).

30. See discussion in Franklin and Anderson, Cases and Materials on Mass Media Law, 4th ed. (Westbury, N.Y.: The Foundation Press, 1990), pp. 600-603 and Goodale and Moodhe, Reporter's Privilege Cases, 2 Communications Law 7 (Practising Law Institute 1988).

31. Rule 17, Rules of Criminal Procedure, Tennessee Court Rules Annotated.

32. Cohen v. Cowles Media Co., 111 S.Ct. 2513.

33. Zurcher v. Stanford Daily, 436 U.S. 519 (1978).

34. Public Law 96-440, 42 U.S.C. 2000aa.

Defamation

Our society places high value on freedom of expression, but society likewise values other personal rights, such as the right to enjoy the good reputation one earns. As noted earlier in this book, the First Amendment is not an absolute, so laws concerning defamation—libel and slander—are not inconsistent with First Amendment guarantees.

Research shows that individuals who think their reputations have been damaged in print or broadcast media usually contact someone at the station or newspaper before talking to a lawyer.[1] What happens at that initial contact can be extremely important in determining whether a libel suit is filed. [See the chapter in this book on "Tips for Avoiding Lawsuits."]

Whether any informal attempts to resolve the issue are undertaken, a Tennessee law specifies that the aggrieved person must ask for a retraction at least five days before filing a civil action for libel.[2] However, the Tennessee Supreme Court has held that failure to give this notice is insufficient grounds to dismiss the case, but it will prevent the plaintiff from receiving punitive damages.[3]

The Libel Defense Resource Center reports that about 90 percent of all libel suits are dropped, dismissed or settled out of court. Although a defamation suit is an immense drain on time and energy, as well as extremely expensive to defend,[4] most news organizations are extremely reluctant to settle out of court for fear of inviting frivolous lawsuits.

Once the suit is filed, both parties engage in discovery proceedings to prepare their cases. Attorneys for each side investigate and take depositions to ascertain the facts of the situation and to gain information about evidence that will be presented during the trial. The discovery process can become extended, involving many hours of expensive legal work.

The defendant might file a motion for summary judgment on any of several grounds. For example, the defendant might argue that no legal wrong has been committed because the offending statements were not defamatory or that the plaintiff will be unable to meet the required burden of proof.[5] If these arguments are persuasive, and if no facts are in dispute, the judge may agree to grant a summary judgment for the defendant, eliminating the need for a trial. This ends the suit unless the plaintiff appeals the ruling to a higher court, arguing that the summary judgment was improperly granted.

If the suit survives preliminary motions and goes to trial, the plaintiff will try to prove that the elements of libel were present. The media defendant will argue that the plaintiff has not been damaged or is otherwise unable to meet the burden of proof. In addition, the defendant will advance one or more legal defenses.

The following sections describe the elements that the plaintiff must prove and the legal defenses for defamation.

Elements of Defamation

A person who sues for libel must prove the following:

- The statement was defamatory.
- The statement caused injury.
- The statement was published.
- The plaintiff was identified in the statement.
- The publisher was at fault in publishing the statement.

Defamatory Meaning

Under Tennessee law, to be actionable as defamatory, a statement must constitute serious threat to the plaintiff's reputation; the words must be reasonably construable as holding the plaintiff up to public hatred, contempt or ridicule, and they must carry with them an element of disgrace.[6] Spoken defamation is slander and written defamation is libel. In most instances, a defamatory statement that is broadcast will be considered libel rather than slander.

The burden of proving that a harmful statement is false is on the plaintiff if he or she is a public official or public figure. In addition, private figures challenging statements that relate to matters of public concern must prove falsity. In a 1978 case the Tennessee Supreme Court held that the plaintiff was not required to prove falsity; rather the defendant could prove that the offending statement was true.[7] But that decision is invalidated by a more recent U.S. Supreme Court ruling that a private figure plaintiff cannot recover damages without also showing the statements at issue are false if the statements relate to matters of public concern.[8]

Historically, libel falls into one of two classifications: libel *per se,* words that are defamatory on their face and thus presumed to damage reputation, and libel *per quod,* words that are not ordinarily defamatory but become damaging because of facts or circumstances extrinsic to the story.

Examples of words that are defamatory on their face include those that falsely accuse someone of committing a crime or of having a loathsome disease. A Tennessee court has held that while it is not actionable to publish accurately that a person has been charged with a crime, it is libelous to add a headline or comments that assume the guilt of the person.[9] However, a claim against Time magazine by James Earl Ray, convicted killer of the Rev. Martin Luther King, Jr., was denied, with the court saying no libel claim existed in newsworthy stories about criminal proceedings involving Ray and in speculation about whether others may have been involved with Ray in the murder.[10]

An example of libel per quod would be to publish an incorrect date for the granting of a divorce so that it appeared that someone had remarried before the divorce became final. As a Tennessee court[11] has noted, the libel *per se* and *per quod* distinctions have little meaning since the U.S. Supreme Court held that states can no longer presume liability without fault.[12] This issue is discussed later in this chapter.

Some states recognize a third category: statements susceptible to two meanings, one defamatory and the other not defamatory. In Tennessee, if a publication is so unambiguous as to reasonably bear but one interpretation, it is for the judge to decide whether it is defamatory. But if the words are capable of more than one interpretation, one of which would render it actionable and the other not, the jury determines which meaning readers would give it.[13]

A Tennessee statute, originally passed in 1858 and amended as late as 1957, makes actionable "any words written, spoken, or printed of a person, wrongfully and maliciously imputing to such person the commission of adultery or fornication."[14] The purpose of the law was to put all imputations of unchastity upon the plane of all other libelous and slanderous charges.[15] A woman who sued after being called a hermaphrodite saw her the case dismissed on the grounds that the statement did not impute an offense involving moral turpitude.[16] Under this section, the fact that the slanderous words were uttered in the heat of passion or anger may mitigate damages.[17]

In most cases involving the mass media, the plaintiff must also prove that the offending statement was false. True statements that harm someone's reputation are not actionable as libel, although in some situations where they are extremely embarrassing, not newsworthy, and highly offensive to reasonable people such statements may be actionable as an invasion of privacy. Thus, to publish accurately that someone has been arrested and charged with murder is not actionable, even though the person subsequently may be acquitted of the charge. Minor inaccuracies will not defeat the defense of truth so long as the part of the statement that carries the sting is true. For example, a libel case would not turn on inaccurately reporting the place of arrest of the murder suspect so long as the suspect was accurately identified and the charge accurately reported.

Injury

The plaintiff must convince the court that the offending statement carried a "sting," meaning that it harmed the plaintiff's reputation. Evidence about a plaintiff's reputation before and after the publication is admissible. In a few instances, courts have decided that plaintiffs were "libel proof" because their reputations were already tarnished beyond the possibility of further damage.[18]

A Tennessee court has held that it is not necessary to prove special damages or out-of-pocket loss in a defamation suit, but there must be material evidence of injury, such as impairment of reputation and standing in the community, personal humiliation and mental anguish and suffering.[19] In the same case, the court ruled that mere anger in response to a telephone call informing the plaintiff of the utterance did not constitute recoverable special damages.

Publication

Publication is usually obvious in cases involving the mass media. Strictly speaking, publication has occurred when at least one person other than the defamed person has received the material. In Tennessee, however, dictation of a libelous letter to a secretary does not constitute a publication for purposes of libel.[20]

In media cases, courts usually have held that publication has not occurred until the material reaches its intended audience. This means that media personnel can discuss a potentially libelous item during the production process without fear of a successful libel suit. A 1988 case in Tennessee held that communication among employees of the same corporation made within the course and scope of their employment relative to duties performed by the corporation are not to be considered as statements published to third persons.[21]

Identification

Identification may be established even though the plaintiff is not named in the story if people reasonably understand that the statement referred to the plaintiff. An address or title might be sufficient to establish identification. In a Tennessee case where two newspapers had edited an angry letter to delete the name of a car dealership, referring to it as "a local import dealer," the court of appeals said "the appropriate test is whether a reasonable third party recipient of the defamatory communication would and did understand it as intended to refer to the plaintiff, not whether the plaintiff himself has an awareness that he is the subject of the communication."[22]

Individuals cannot sue successfully just because they are members of a large group that has been defamed. For example, a statement that "all lawyers are crooks" would not be sufficient identification for an individual lawyer to sustain a suit, but an attorney might be able to prove individual identification and harm by the statement that "all lawyers at the XYZ Law Firm are crooks." In the Tennessee case referred to in the previous paragraph, the car dealer plaintiff argued that deletion of his name was insufficient to avoid identifying him because there were only two "local import dealers" in town. However, the court said that since there were two import dealers in town, readers would not know which one was referred to in the letter. More significantly, the court said, the letter referred to "used" cars, and there were a number of dealers in the area who sold used foreign cars. The court also noted that the meaning of the word "local" was imprecise and helped veil the identity of the plaintiffs.[23] The appeals court said that a different result could have been reached if the plaintiffs had introduced testimony at trial from readers who claimed to have understood that the letter referred to the plaintiff's car dealership.

No exact number exists for how small a group must be before any single member can claim to have been damaged enough to sustain a libel suit. A "rule of 25" grew out of a libel case during the 1950s, but subsequent court decisions allowed members of groups larger than 25 to sue when individuals were closely identified with the group.

Although published statements may identify and damage the memory of a deceased person, in Tennessee, as in other states, the estate cannot sue.[24] If a plaintiff in Tennessee dies after a favorable judgment in a slander suit that is pending on appeal, the action is not abated.[25] However, if the judgment on appeal goes against the deceased plaintiff, the suit is abated as though no judgment had been obtained.[26]

Fault

Fault joined the list of elements that a libel plaintiff had to prove when the U.S. Supreme Court determined that the Constitution protected defamatory statements when they were published without fault. Before the 1964 Supreme Court ruling in *New York Times v. Sullivan,*[27] after a libel plaintiff had established publication, identification and defamation, the burden of proof shifted to the defendant to offer a defense. The various categories of libel plaintiffs and the amount of fault each has to prove is explained below in the section discussing the constitutional defense.

Defenses Against Libel

Media defendants will attempt to persuade the court that they should not have to pay damages for a libelous statement because its publication was protected by the Constitution or one of the traditional common law defenses.

The Constitutional Defense

What It Means

Before 1964, libel was considered outside the protection of the Constitution. Unless the false, defamatory statement could be defended under common law, the defendant despite the best of intentions and news gathering efforts was liable for damages.

A full-page advertisement in the *New York Times* led to a case that profoundly altered libel law. The ad criticized police and public officials in several cities for tactics used to disrupt the civil rights movement and sought contributions to pay bail for movement leaders who had been jailed for their protest activities. Accusations made in the advertisement were true for the most part, but the copy contained several rather minor factual errors. L. B. Sullivan, police commissioner in Montgomery, Ala., sued the New York Times for libel. He won $500,000 for damages in the state courts of Alabama, but the Supreme Court of the United States overturned the damage award.

In *New York Times v. Sullivan* the Supreme Court reasoned that public officials must live with the risks of a political system in which there is "a profound national commitment to the principle that debate on public issues should be uninhibited, robust, and wide-open, and that it may well include vehement, caustic, and sometimes unpleasantly sharp attacks on government or public officials." Further, the Court said that "erroneous statement is inevitable in free debate, and . . . it must be protected if the freedoms of expression are to have the breathing space that they need to survive."[28]

Standards of Fault

The Court said the Constitution protected false, defamatory statements about public officials, provided that the defendant did not publish such statements recklessly or knowingly. On the basis of that ruling, public officials, in order to win a libel case, were obligated to prove that a media defendant was at fault.

Actual malice, the standard of fault specified by the Court, was defined as knowledge of falsity or reckless disregard for truth. Soon afterward, the Court determined that, to win a libel suit, public figures, in addition to public officials, should prove that the defendant published with knowledge that the defamatory statements were false or with reckless disregard for truth.

Neither the U.S. Supreme Court nor the Tennessee courts have set forth a single definition of "reckless disregard." In fact, the Supreme Court has said that the term "cannot be fully encompassed in one infallible definition; . . . inevitably its outer limits will be marked out through case-by-case adjudication, as is true with so many legal standards for judging concrete cases."[29]

Tennessee courts, in determining whether actual malice was present, have followed the Supreme Court's lead in considering whether the publisher had "reasonable doubts as to falsity."[30] Other factors include

- the number and credibility of sources,
- time constraints involved in gathering information, writing and editing the story, and
- the reasonable probability that the information was accurate.

In a 1974 case,[31] the Supreme Court, holding that states could no longer impose liability without fault, extended to all libel plaintiffs the burden of proving the defendant published with fault. Each state was free to set its own fault standard for private plaintiffs; however, the Court said that all libel plaintiffs would have to prove actual malice in order to win punitive damages.

Negligence, the fault standard in Tennessee for private individuals,[32] has been defined somewhat differently from state to state. The Tennessee Supreme Court said that in determining the issue of liability, "the conduct of the defendant is to be measured against what a reasonably prudent person would, or would not, have done under the same or similar circumstances. . . . In our opinion, the appropriate question to be determined from a preponderance of the evidence is whether the defendant exercised reasonable care and caution in checking on the truth or falsity and the defamatory character of the communication before publishing it."[33] In answering this question, the jury can rely on its own experience and instincts to determine whether an ordinarily prudent person would have behaved as publisher did.[34] Some states use the "reasonable publisher" definition of negligence whether a reasonable publisher in the same community or a similar community under existing circumstances would have published the defamatory statement.[35]

Plaintiff's Status: Public or Private

As the fault standard depends on the status of the plaintiff, the outcome of a libel case often hinges on whether the plaintiff is considered a public official or figure or a private person. This is not always easy to determine, and many libel verdicts have been overturned by appeals courts on the basis that the wrong fault standard was imposed on the plaintiff. In a series of cases debating this issue, the courts have set down these guidelines for deciding the status of the plaintiff:

> A **public official** is one who has, or who the public perceives to have, substantial responsibility for or control over the conduct of governmental affairs.[36] A government employee does not necessarily meet this definition.

In a 1978 decision, the Tennessee Supreme Court quoted the public official definition in the previous paragraph but added that the label "does not necessarily apply only to high public position. Any position of employment that carries with it duties and responsibilities affecting the lives, liberty, money or property of a citizen or that may enhance or disrupt his enjoyment of life, his peace and tranquility, or that of his family, is a public office within the meaning of the constitutional privilege."[37] In this case, a junior-ranking social worker sued a Johnson City newspaper that had published that she had "coerced [another woman] into submitting to sterilization" in order to regain custody of her children who were in foster homes. The Tennessee court of appeals had held that the social worker was not a public official, but the state supreme court reversed, holding that to the family involved, the social worker "was the very epitome of government."[38]

In *Gertz v. Welch,*[39] the U.S. Supreme Court distinguished two different types of public figures:

> **All-purpose public figures** are people who achieve such pervasive fame or notoriety or who may occupy positions of such persuasive power and influence that they are considered public figures for all purposes and in all contexts. An all-purpose public figure would be someone with a high degree of name recognition in the community.

Limited public figures are persons who by their public statements and actions have projected themselves into the arena of public controversy and into the very vortex of the discussion of a question of pressing public concern in an attempt to influence the resolution of an issue.

Few public figures are "all-purpose" public figures in that they are involved in all aspects of public life. Instead, most are limited public figures; they voluntarily become involved in just a few, perhaps only one, controversy. For example, someone who becomes involved in the public debate about whether abortion should be legal in the United States would be a public figure in a libel suit concerning that particular controversy. However, if that same person filed a libel suit about a private matter or a public controversy in which he or she had not become involved voluntarily, that person would be classified as a private person and in Tennessee would seek to argue that the publisher acted with negligence rather than actual malice, which is more difficult to prove. Another example: A person involved in a highly publicized divorce case was held to be a private person in a libel case that originated when a magazine misstated the grounds for granting the divorce. The court held that divorce was a private matter, not a public controversy.[40]

Private person: one who, although perhaps well known in the community, has no authority or responsibility for the conduct of governmental affairs and has not thrust himself or herself into the middle of an important public controversy.

Elmer Gertz, the plaintiff in *Gertz v. Welch,* was a prominent lawyer who was widely known in several contexts in Chicago. As a lawyer, he had represented defendants in highly publicized cases; he was an author and an amateur actor and had served on various citizens' committees in Chicago. The libel case arose after Gertz agreed to represent a family in a civil suit against a Chicago police officer who had been found guilty of murder in the shooting of a youth. A John Birch Society magazine then published an article falsely accusing Gertz of having a criminal record and being a "Leninist" or a "Communist fronter." Despite his prominence, the Supreme Court ruled that Gertz was a private person for the purposes of his suit because he had done nothing to inject himself into the controversy surrounding the shooting and subsequent criminal trial of the policeman, which was the focus of the magazine article. In representing the family in a civil action, Gertz was just practicing his profession and acting in the capacity of a private person, the Court held.

Tennessee courts[41] have relied upon an analysis of public figure as set forth by the 6th Circuit Court of Appeals, which handles federal appeals from Tennessee. In a case that originated in Tennessee, the 6th Circuit court used a two-step analysis in determining whether a plaintiff was a public figure: First, decide whether a public controversy exists. Second, determine the nature and extent of the plaintiff's participation in that public controversy by examining three factors:[42]

- the extent to which participation in the controversy is voluntary,
- the extent to which there is access to channels of effective communication in order to counteract false statements, and
- the prominence of the role played in the public controversy."

Neutral Reportage

Neutral reportage is recognized in a few jurisdictions as protection in a libel action. Neutral reportage refers to the practice of accurately and disinterestedly reporting that a responsible, prominent person or organization made false, defamatory statements about a public official or public figure. No reported cases in Tennessee have dealt with this issue.

Courts that have recognized neutral reportage as a libel defense have accepted the argument that such accusations are newsworthy and that the First Amendment does not require the press to ignore newsworthy statements just because the press cannot verify them or just because the reporter has doubts about their truth. In cases where the doctrine has been accepted, the allegedly defamatory stories included denials or explanations from the defamed parties.

Common Law Defenses

Libel defendants will advance the constitutional defense if the published statement is false but was published with insufficient fault to win damages. In addition, defendants may argue one or more of the common law defenses: fair comment, qualified privilege or truth.

Fair Comment

In a 1990 decision, the Supreme Court held that the Constitution does not provide a "wholesale defamation exemption for anything that might be labeled opinion."[43] However, the common law defense of fair comment protects opinion about matters of public interest or things that have been put on public display. Fair comment and criticism allows reviewers, for example, to publish scathing reviews of things such as plays, movies, books, and restaurants.

Tennessee precedent makes clear that the doctrine of fair comment applies to statements of opinion rather than factual statements.[44] If opinion relies for its support upon the existence of undisclosed information, such information must be accurate. For example, it is protected opinion to say that an actor gave a poor performance in a play, but to falsely imply that the poor performance was attributable to the actor's use of drugs is an unprotected statement of fact.

A newspaper is responsible for what it publishes, including letters to the editor. Like editorials, the letter writer's opinions are protected by fair comment, but the facts that underpin opinions are not protected if they are false and defamatory. A Tennessee court of appeals upheld a summary judgment in favor of a newspaper after determining that a letter to the editor had been edited to avoid specific references to the plaintiff and that such editing sufficiently indicated a lack of negligence.[45]

Privilege

Privilege protects defamatory statements made during certain public settings such as judicial, legislative or administrative meetings, and it also protects reporting about such statements. Tennessee courts have held that statements made during such public meetings are privileged as long as they are relevant and pertinent to the matters being discussed.[46] They cannot be the basis of a defamation action, even if they are false, known to be false, or malicious.[47]

The rationale for the privilege is that societal interests will best be served if people involved in deciding public issues, including citizens, are able to engage in robust and open debate without fear of being sued for defamation.[40] The term "privilege" sometimes causes confusion because, obviously, no one has the privilege to defame someone else. "Immunity" would be a more precise term. The law recognizes two types of privilege: absolute and qualified, with the latter also referred to as "conditional" privilege.

Parties involved in legislative, judicial, or executive proceedings—for example, members of legislative bodies, judges, trial participants, and others carrying out the duties of their public offices – have absolute privilege. The media have qualified privilege allowing them to report on privileged situations, with the privilege conditioned upon an accurate and complete or a fair abridgement of the proceedings.

Usually, to be considered privileged, the proceeding must be open to the public, or the information must be available for public inspection. Public meetings and public records are examples of privileged situations. It is this common law defense, for example, that allows the media to cover damaging and false statements that are made during trials. Even if it is later revealed that a witness lied during testimony, the media are not held liable for repeating those lies. The privilege applies only to those comments made during the proceedings, however, not to comments made by parties outside the proceedings.

Questions arise about what proceeding are covered by privilege. Generally the privilege applies to meetings involving public interest, not private meetings, although meetings of medical societies and bar associations and private meetings open to the public have been held privileged.[49] An old case in Tennessee extended privilege to a public meetings unrelated to governing. There the court granted the privilege to a person who during a church service produced evidence that supported his previous accusation that another person killed two horses.[50] Cases recognizing qualified privilege for the media in Tennessee have dealt with judicial proceedings,[51] legislative proceedings[52] and a public hearing of a board of zoning appeals.[53]

In Tennessee, qualified privilege protects publishing the contents of pleadings filed in court even though no judicial action has been taken, provided that the publication is made without malice.[54] Tennessee differs in this regard from most states in that qualified privilege generally does not apply until some action has been taken on a lawsuit.[55] The purpose is to prevent a person from filing a suit containing false and defamatory charges about an enemy and then promptly withdrawing the suit after damaging publicity. The facts of the case in which the Tennessee Supreme Court adopted the minority principle, which overruled dictum in a previous Tennessee case,[56] were somewhat out of the ordinary in that the person suing for defamation was the same person who had filed the original pleadings. In that particular case, the plaintiff filed a defamation suit against a student humor magazine at Vanderbilt University and then filed another suit against the Vanderbilt student newspaper after it reported the original filing and reproduced much of the allegedly defamatory material, which was included in the pleadings.

Where parties have a common interest, Tennessee courts have applied privilege conditioned upon absence of malice. For example, where a corporation foreman reported to his manager that an employee had stolen a book of tickets redeemable for ice, the court held that the foreman and manager had in common the financial interests of the corporation.[57] The same rationale was applied where a supervising nurse reported the behavior of another nurse to hospital authorities.[58]

Truth

As falsity is an integral part of the definition of defamation, truth is the best defense against libel. Although public figures and officials and where the offending statement concerns public matters even private figure plaintiffs have the burden of proving falsity—certainly a heavy burden—the defendant will try to convince the jury that the published statements were true.

The truth must be as broad as the charge. To support a published charge that the plaintiff is a crook, it is not enough to prove, for example, that he once shortchanged someone. Likewise, to prove that the plaintiff was convicted of a misdemeanor shoplifting charge is insufficient as a defense if the published statement said the plaintiff was a convicted felon. Courts usually will allow truth to stand as a defense even though the story contains minor inaccuracies that do not carry the "sting" of the statement. For example, to publish that someone was arrested on Aug. 1 instead of Aug. 2 is unlikely to defeat the truth defense unless other circumstances make the exact date important to the case.

In Tennessee, a newspaper's motion to dismiss a libel charge was reversed on appeals and a new trial ordered for a news story that was literally true but which, because of omitted facts, left the false impression that the plaintiff was involved in an adulterous affair.[59] Based on information from a police report form, the *Memphis Press-Scimitar* published that Mrs. Ruth A. Nichols was treated at a hospital for a bullet wound after a shooting at her home and that another woman was being held by police in connection with the shooting. The story continued: "Officers said the incident took place Thursday night after the suspect arrived at the Nichols home and found her husband there with Mrs. Nichols."[60] Key information absent from the police report and subsequent newspaper story was that both Mr. and Mrs. Nichols, the assailant's husband, and two other people were sitting in the living room of the Nicholas home when the shooting occurred. At trial, Mr. and Mrs. Nichols had argued that the reporter failed to use reasonable care and thus was negligent in relying on the police report alone and not talking with police officers or taking other steps to gather information for the story.

Other Considerations in Defamation Suits

Retraction

A retraction is not a libel defense, but it may be sufficient to ward off a suit, or, if a suit is successful, a retraction may mitigate damages. The Tennessee retraction statute[61] provides that notice must be given at least five days before filing any civil action for libel. If a periodical publishes a retraction within ten days after receiving the notice or in the next issue if greater than ten days, and if at trial it appears that the article "was published in good faith, that its falsity was due to an honest mistake of the facts, and that there were reasonable grounds for believing that the statements in the article were true," then the plaintiff may not recover punitive damages. The statute makes no mention of broadcast media, and, interestingly, the exemption from punitive damages does not apply to articles "about or affecting" a candidate for political office that is published within ten days before the election.[62]

In a 1949 case concerning the adequacy of a retraction, the Tennessee Court of Appeals said that to mitigate damages, a retraction should use unambiguous language, admit the defamatory statement was unfounded and made without proper information, offer the regrets and apology of the publisher and should be frank, fair and unequivocal and should not be mixed with an attempted justification.[63]

Statute of Limitations

The statute of limitations in Tennessee is one year for a libel case[64] and six months for slander.[65]

Exemption for Broadcasting

Tennessee law provides an exemption for broadcast station owners, licensees, or operators and their employees for on-air defamatory statements made by someone else unless it can be shown that station personnel "failed to exercise due care to prevent the publication or utterance of such statement."[66] The statute specifies that the burden of proof is on the station to show "due care."

Both state and federal laws provide that broadcast stations are not liable for damages for defamatory statements made by candidates for public office, unless the statement is made by an agent or employee of the station during the course of employment.[67]

Exemption for Commercial Printers

Commercial printers who have no role in writing or editing copy are exempt from libel actions unless the material is libelous *per se* or the printer or employees knew or "in the exercise of ordinary care should have known" that the material was false.[68] The Tennessee statute also requires that commercial printers keep a permanent record of the name and address of the person providing the copy and to furnish such information, if requested in writing, to the person allegedly libeled.

Criminal Libel

Until 1989, Tennessee, like many states, had a criminal libel statute making it a misdemeanor to publish "a malicious defamation of a person . . . intending to provoke him to wrath, or expose him to public hatred, contempt, or ridicule, or to deprive him of the benefits of public confidence and social intercourse; or any malicious defamation made public as aforesaid, designed to blacken and vilify the memory of one who is dead, and tending to scandalize or provoke his surviving relatives or friends."[69] The jury had the right to determine the law and the facts,[70] and truth was a defense.[71]

An example of criminal libel in Tennessee is a 1961 case[72] where a newspaper published a letter by a police chief accusing a district attorney general of using "Hitler-like tactics" to conduct investigations. The state supreme court held that this constituted criminal libel under Tennessee law because the letter questioned the administration of public justice in such a way as to injure or hurt its administration. In that same case, the court held that language must be libelous *per se* to constitute criminal libel.

When the Tennessee Criminal Sentencing Reform Act of 1989 rewrote the entire state criminal code, no provision was made for criminal libel.

Endnotes

1. Randall P. Bezanson, Gilbert Cranberg, and John Soloski, *Libel Law and the Press: Myth and Reality* (New York: The Free Press, 1987).

2. T.C.A. 29-24-103.

3. Langford v. Vanderbilt University, 287 S.W.2d 32, 199 Tenn. 389 (1956). In Memphis Publishing Co. v. Nichols, 569 S.W.2d 412 (1978), the Tennessee Supreme Court noted the effect of *Gertz* on the retraction statute in that punitive damages cannot be awarded absent a showing of actual malice.

4. A 1991 study put the average cost of defending a libel suit through a trial at $175,000. That does not include additional expenses for appeals or damages if the defendant loses the suit. John Soloski and Randall Bezanson, "Libel Law and Journalistic Malpractice: A Preliminary Analysis of Fault in Libel Litigation," paper presented at the Association for Education in Journalism and Mass Communication annual convention, August 1991. The Libel Defense Resourse Center reported that the average jury award for libel in 1990 and 1991 was $9 million, an increase from the $1.5 million average recorded during the decade of the 1980s.

5. In Tennessee, a public figure plaintiff must be able to show actual malice with "convincing clarity" to defeat a motion for summary judgment. Trigg v. Lakeway Publishers, Inc., 720 S.W.2d 69 (Tenn. Ct. App. 1986).

6. Katahn v. Hearst Corp. 742 F.Supp. 437 (M.D. Tenn, 1990).

7. Memphis Publishing Co. v. Nichols, 569 S.W.2d 412 (1978).

8. Philadelphia Newspapers Inc. v. Hepps, 475 U.S. 767 (1986).

9. Commercial Pub. Co. v. Smith, 149 F.704, 79 C.C.A. 410 (1907).

10. Ray v. Time, Inc., 452 F.Supp. 618, affirmed 582 F.2d 1280.

11. Memphis Publishing Co. v. Nichols, 569 S.W.2d 412 (Tenn. 1978).

12. Gertz. v. Robert Welch, Inc., 418 U.S. 323.

13. Dupont Eng'g Co. v. Nashville Banner Publishing Co., 13 F.2d 186 (M.D. Tenn 1925).

14. T.C.A. 29-4-101.

15. Cohen v. Pinson, 1 Tenn. Civ. App. 93 (1910).

16. Huckaby v. Winchester, 7 Tenn. Civ. App. 66 (1917).

17. Hackett v. Brown, 49 Tenn 264 (1870).

18. See, e.g. Cardillo v. Doubleday, 518 F.2d 638 (2d Cir. 1975), Logan v. District of Columbia, 447 F.Supp. 1328 (D.D.C. 1978) and Jackson v. Longcope, 476 N.E.2d 617 (Mass. 1985).

19. Handley v. May, 588 S.W.2d 772 (Tenn. App. 1979).

20. Freeman v. Dayton Scale Co., 159 Tenn. 413 (1929); Insurance Research Service, Inc. v. Associates Finance Corp., 134 F. Supp. 54 (M.D. Tenn. 1955).

21. Woods v. Helmi, 758 S.W.2d 219 (Tenn. App., 1988). This case involved a supervisor's memo to hospital officials concerning the operating room behavior of a certified registered nurse anesthetist who subsequently was fired.

22. Stones River Motors Inc. v. Mid-South Publishing Co., Inc., 651 S.W.2d at 718 (Tenn. App. 1983).

23. Stones River Motors Inc. v. Mid-South Publishing Co., Inc., 651 S.W.2d at 717-718 (Tenn. App. 1983).

24. Memphis Development Foundation v. Factors Etc., Inc., 616 F.2d 956, cert. denied 101 S.Ct. 358 (C.A. Tenn. 1980).

25. Akers v. Akers, 84 Tenn. 7 (1885).

26. Id.

27. New York Times v. Sullivan, 376 U.S. 254 (1964).

28. Id. at 271-272.

29. St. Amant v. Thompson, 390 U.S. 727 (1968).

30. Trigg v. Lakeway Publishers Inc., 720 S.W.2d 69 (Tenn. App. 1986).

31. Gertz. v. Robert Welch, Inc., 418 U.S. 323. Tennessee courts have made clear that the doctrine of presumed damages in libel and slander cases is no longer applicable, e.g. Emerson v. Garner, 732 S.W.2d 613 (Tenn. App. 1987).

32. Memphis Publishing Co. v. Nichols, 569 S.W.2d 412 (Tenn. 1978).

33. Id. at 418.

34. Id.

35. e.g. Gobin v. Globe Pub. Co. 219 Kan. 223 (Kansas 1975).

36. Rosenblatt v. Baer, 383 U.S. 75 at 85 (1966).

37. Press Inc. v. Verran, 569 S.W.2d 435 at 441 (Tenn. 1978).

38. Id. at 443.

39. 418 U.S. 323 (1974).

40. Time Inc. v. Firestone, 424 U.S. 448 (1976).

41. Cloyd v. Press Inc., 629 S.W.2d 24 (Tenn. App. 1981) and Trigg v. Lakeway Publishers Inc., 720 S.W.2d 69 (Tenn. App. 1986).

42. Street v. National Broadcasting Co., 645 F.2d at 1234 (1981) cert. granted, 454 U.S. 815, appeal dismissed, 454 U.S. 1095 (1981).

43. Milkovich v. Lorain Journal, 110 S.Ct. 2695.

44. Venn v. Tennessean Newspapers, Inc. 201 F.Supp. 47 (M.D. Tenn 1962), affirmed 313 F.2d 639, cert. denied 83 S.Ct. 1872.

45. Stones River Motors Inc. v. Mid-South Publishing Co., Inc., 651 S.W.2d at 718 (Tenn. App. 1983).

46. Evans v. Nashville Banner Pub. Co., 15 Media Law Reporter 2216, 1988 WESTLAW 105718 at 4 (Tenn. App. 1988), citing Wells v. Carter, 164 Tenn. 400, 402-03, 50 S.W.2d 228, 229 (1932) (judicial proceedings); Logan's Super Mkts., Inc. v. McCalla, 208 Tenn. 68, 72-74, 343 S.W.2d 892, 894 (1961) (legislative proceedings); Langford v. Vanderbilt Univ., 44 Tenn.App. 694, 706, 318 S.W.2d 568, 574 (1958) (legislative and judicial proceedings).

47. Evans v. Nashville Banner Pub. Co., 15 Media Law Reporter 2216, 1988 WESTLAW 105718 at 4 (Tenn. App. 1988), citing Jones v. Trice, 210 Tenn. 535, 548, 360 S.W.2d 48, 54 (1962).

48. Logan's Super Mkts., Inc. v. McCalla, 208 Tenn. at 73, 343 S.W.2d at 89; Boody v. Garrison, 636 S.W.2d 715, 717 (Tenn.Ct.App.1981); see also W. Keeton, Prosser and Keeton on the Law of Torts § 114 (5th ed. 1984).

49. Prosser, Torts 623 (2d ed. 1955).

50. Dunn v. Winters, 21 Tenn. 512 (1841).

51. American Publishing Co. v. Gamble, 90 S.W.2d 1005 (1906), Wells v. Carter, 164 Tenn. 400, 402-03, 50 S.W.2d 228, 229 (1932), Black v. Nashville Banner Pub. Co., 141 S.W.2d 908 (1939).

52. Logan's Super Mkts., Inc. v. McCalla, 208 Tenn. 68, 72-74, 343 S.W.2d 892, 894 (1961).

53. Evans v. Nashville Banner Pub. Co., 15 Media Law Reporter 2216, 1988 WESTLAW 105718 (Tenn. App. 1988).

54. Langford v. Vanderbilt University, 287 S.W.2d 32, 199 Tenn. 389 (1956).

55. Prosser, Torts 2d 624 (1955). For more discussion of this issue, see Donald F. Paine, "Conditional Privilege in Tennessee," 30 Tenn. L. R. 569 (1963).

56. American Publishing Co. v. Gamble, 90 S.W.2d 1005 (1906).

57. Southern Ice Co. v. Black, 189 S.W. 861 (1916)

58. Woods v. Helmi, 758 S.W.2d 219 (Tenn. App., 1988).

59. Memphis Publishing Co. v. Nichols, 569 S.W.2d 412 (1978).

60. Id. at 414.

61. T.C.A. 29-24-103.

62. T.C.A. 29-24-103(b)(2).

63. Knoxville Pub. Co. v. Taylor, 215 S.W.2d 27.

64. T.C.A. 28-3-104

65. T.C.A. 28-3-103.

66. T.C.A. 29-24-104.

67. Id. (c).

68. T.C.A. 29-4-104.
69. T.C.A. 39-2-401.
70. T.C.A. 39-2-403.
71. T.C.A. 39-2-404.
72. State v. Guinn, 208 Tenn. 527.

Privacy

The law of privacy in the United States is relatively new in comparison with defamation law. It wasn't until the 20th Century that a person's right to be free from unwarranted publicity was acknowledged by either statutory or common law.

Whereas defamation law is designed to protect reputation, privacy law protects one's right to be left alone and to be free from mental anguish caused by unwarranted publicity.

Four Privacy Torts

Today most states recognize four distinct torts, known collectively as invasion of privacy. As listed in the *Restatement of the Law, 2d, Torts*,[1] these legal wrongs are as follows:

- Appropriation of another's name or likeness;
- Unreasonable intrusion upon the seclusion of another;
- Unreasonable publicity given to another's private life;
- Publicity that unreasonably places another in a false light.

Tennessee courts have not expressly recognized[2] a common law right of privacy and have considered very few cases dealing with privacy; however, federal courts in Tennessee have decided cases as though the four privacy torts existed in the state. In 1984 the state legislature passed a statute[3] protecting against unauthorized appropriation. As there is little case law to draw on in Tennessee, much of the explanation of the four privacy areas that follows comes from rulings from other states and from the federal courts.

Appropriation

Generally, appropriation claims against the mass media have involved advertising departments at periodicals or broadcast stations, rather than news-editorial departments. Appropriation, including the closely related "right of publicity," is the one privacy area for which Tennessee statutorily has created a cause of action. The Personal Rights Protection Act of 1984 creates for every individual a property right in the use of his name, photograph, or likeness in any medium in any manner.[4] The act makes it a Class C misdemeanor[5] and also subject to civil action to knowingly use or infringe upon the use of another individual's name or likeness "as an item of commerce for purposes of advertising products, merchandise, goods, or services, or for purposes of fund raising, solicitation of donations, purchases of products, merchandise, goods, or services" without prior consent.[6]

Extensive litigation surrounding merchandising of Elvis Presley's name and likeness after his death and efforts by the Presley estate to control the such uses provided the impetus for legislative action in Tennessee to create a right of publicity. Generally, a personal right unlike a property right does not continue after death. In its attempts to prevent unauthorized commercial use of Presley's name or picture, his heirs received conflicting results in courts in different jurisdictions.[7] By creating a property right in one's name and likeness and making that right descendible, the Tennessee statute enabled Presley's heirs to control the use of his name or likeness, at least within the state of Tennessee. As of 1991, at least seven other states had passed laws creating a property right to publicity surviving death.[8] Under the Tennessee Personal Rights Protection Act of 1984, an estate has the right to assign and license a name or likeness for an indefinite number of years so long as there is no two-year-long period of non-use. The non-use period does not apply during the first 10 years after the individual's death.[9]

Although print and broadcast media are commercial vehicles designed to yield monetary profits, the use of an individual's name in a newsworthy context without consent is not considered an appropriation for commercial purposes. Tennessee's Personal Rights Protection Act of 1984 specifically notes this exemption.[10] In fact, courts have held that it is not actionable as appropriation for the media to reuse for promotional purposes names or pictures that they have published previously in a newsworthy context. For example, football star Joe Namath was denied his claim for damages against *Sports Illustrated* after the magazine showed a previously published picture of Namath in an advertisement for subscriptions. The court held that the magazine was merely providing a sample of its typical contents and that this amounted to incidental advertising rather than for purposes of trade.[11] Care must be taken with such promotional pieces, however, so that they do not state or imply that the individual is endorsing the periodical or broadcast station.

Although broadcast stations may use brief film clips of commercial performances such as sporting events without prior permission, they must not air so much that the commercial value is diminished for the performer or owner of the event. A Scripps Howard television station in Ohio was found guilty of appropriation for showing a 15-second tape of a "human cannonball" act. The tape was broadcast on the evening news program as a news item about a county fair. Hugo Zacchini successfully argued that his right to publicity and his right to make a living were harmed because that 15 seconds effectively included his entire act, making it unnecessary for people to pay to attend the fair to see the act.[12]

The use of a name alone generally is not sufficient to sustain an appropriation suit. Rather a particular person's identity must be used. Thus, no cause of action exists for an individual who happens to have the same name as another person who consented to have the name used in a commercial sense.

Appropriation claims have arisen over the use of celebrity "look-alikes" or "sound-alikes" hired to promote products or services. New York law was applied in most of these suits because New York City advertising agencies were involved, and the celebrity plaintiffs have won where there existed the likelihood of consumer confusion about the involvement of a celebrity.[13]

Defense against Appropriation

Consent is the defense against the appropriation privacy tort. Although implied consent has been recognized in some courts, a written release is better protection. It is important that the person giving permission is legally able to enter in contractual agreements. Minors or mentally incompetent adults can not do so.

In addition, the consent should be as broad as the eventual use of the name or likeness. For example, a photographer needs a release form that grants permission not only to take the photograph but also to publish it. Consent may prove to be insufficient as a defense if a photograph is substantially altered. For example, a model gave consent for a picture of her lying in bed reading a book to be used to advertise educational books. She successfully sued for appropriation after the picture was altered significantly, including the addition of a racy title for the book she was reading, and used to advertise bed sheets.[14]

In the only reported case in Tennessee regarding consent for the use of a person's likeness for commercial purposes,[15] the Tennessee Supreme Court held that where a woman consented to the use of her picture on a club bulletin board, she effectively waived her right of privacy with respect to the photograph and had no cause of action when the club subsequently used it in a newspaper advertisement. It should be noted that this decision was handed down in 1967, before the Tennessee General Assembly passed the Personal Rights Protection Act of 1984.

Intrusion

The privacy tort known as intrusion or trespass concerns the conduct of journalists while gathering information, rather than the nature of the material published. Publication is not an essential element of this legal wrong.

According to the Restatement of Torts, "one who intentionally intrudes, physically or otherwise, upon the solitude or seclusion of another or his private affairs or concerns is subject to liability to the other for invasion of his privacy, if the intrusion would be highly offensive to a reasonable person."[16]

Reasonable Expectation of Privacy

There must be a reasonable expectation of privacy in order for an intrusion claim to be successful. One should have no reasonable expectation of privacy for acts conducted in public or that can be viewed from a public place. For example, plaintiffs were unsuccessful in their intrusion claims for photographs taken and published in the following situations:

- front-page photo of plaintiffs' home with a caption saying that the home was "weatherworn and unkept";[17]
- a man standing in line at unemployment office to assist someone else in filing for unemployment compensation, but

photo left the impression that the plaintiff was seeking to collect unemployment payment;[18]

- a nude woman, shielding her body with a small towel, photographed while running across a parking lot after having been held hostage.[19]

In the 1956 case in which the Tennessee Supreme Court indirectly recognized a common law right of privacy, the court held that plaintiffs should have had no expectation of privacy concerning material included as part of their pleadings in a defamation action. By their filing of the action, the court held, the plaintiffs made its contents a matter of public record.[20]

The U. S. Supreme Court has ruled that one should have no expectation of privacy for abandoned property, such as garbage, left in public places.[21]

An undercover police officer should have no expectation of privacy while carrying out official duties, a court ruled.[22] The officer was filmed during an encounter with a lingerie model at a massage parlor after the owner of the massage parlor, who said he was being harassed by local police, arranged for television cameras to secretly film the encounter.

While the general rule is that anything visible from a public place can be legally photographed, photographers who are overly aggressive in pursuing their subjects may be fined or enjoined on general nuisance or harassment statutes. Such was the case for a free-lance photographer who spent years hounding Jacqueline Kennedy Onassis and the Kennedy children. The Secret Service convinced a judge to issue an injunction ordering the photographer to remain a specified distance from members of the Kennedy family.[23]

Newsgathering on Private Property

Courts have held that the First Amendment accords newsmen no "immunity from torts or crimes committed during the course of newsgathering."[24] The mass media have settled out of court or lost intrusion cases for newsgathering activities conducted on privately owned property that was open to the public especially where cameras or tape recorders were used.

The fact that a restaurant is open to the public does not excuse a camera crew working on a story about health-code violations from entering the restaurant with lights on and cameras running, interrupting the normal course of business.[25] The fact that reporters were cooperating with law-enforcement officials was no defense when a non-licensed, quack doctor won an intrusion suit against Life magazine after two reporters were permitted access to his home under the pretense of seeking medical advice. Information reporters obtained by using a hidden camera and tape recorder was used to help convict the man of practicing medicine without a license, but a court held the reporters guilty of illegal trespass.[26]

Cases are mixed on the question of whether the press may safely accompany officials onto private property during an official investigation. A Florida newspaper successfully defended an intrusion case by arguing that its photographer was protected by "common custom and usage" and implied consent when he accompanied a fire marshall into a private residence during an investigation of a fatal fire.[27] The owner of the home was not present, and the photographer entered at the invitation of the fire marshall and even contributed photos to the investigation. The common custom and usage and implied consent argument was denied by a New York court where television reporters and photographers were sued for accompanying a humane society investigator into a house to execute a search warrant.[28] The fact situation in the New York case was distinguished from the Florida case by the presence of the property owner and her request that the journalists not enter her home.

In another case[29] reporters were found guilty of criminal trespass for entering private property without consent for news gathering purposes. While this Oklahoma case was not a civil suit for invasion of privacy, it makes the point that the First Amendment provides no shield for news gathering on private property. Reporters had accompanied demonstrators onto the grounds of a nuclear power plant construction site rather than viewing the scheduled protest from a viewing area established by the plant operators.

Defenses Against Intrusion Claim

Consent, either expressed or implied, is the best defense against an intrusion claim. In addition, the defendant can try to persuade a court that the plaintiff should have had no reasonable expectation of privacy or that the intrusion was not highly offensive to a reasonable person. For example, it would not be considered offensive to knock on the door to someone's private residence or to interrupt someone's solitude with a telephone call. Such interruptions, if clearly unwelcomed and made repeatedly, might reach the required level of offensiveness.

Publication of Private Information

The *Restatement* defines this invasion of privacy tort as giving "publicity to a matter concerning the private life of another . . . if the matter publicized is of a kind that (a) would be highly offensive to a reasonable person and (b) is not of legitimate concern to the public."[30]

Publicity Element

Generally, to be actionable, the highly offensive private information must be communicated to the public at large rather than simply a third individual, as in libel. Courts have held that the publicity element was not met where private information about a student's grades[31] or a plaintiff's debt[32] was communicated to someone or some group with a specific need to know. The number of people reached, not the form of the communication, is the important factor.

Highly Offensive to a Reasonable Person

Embarrassment and humiliation are not sufficient to support the claim of publication of private information. One court said that the conduct must be "so outrageous or atrocious as to exceed all possible bounds of decency."[33] The tort is not designed to protect the "overly sensitive." In addition, public figures may expect greater scrutiny than private individuals. One court noted: "Revelations may be so intimate and so unwarranted in view of the victim's position as to outrage the community's notions of decency. But when focused upon public characters, truthful comments, upon dress, speech habits, and the ordinary aspects of personality will usually not transgress this line. Regrettably or not, the misfortunes and frailties of neighbors and public figures are subjects of considerable interest and discussion to the rest of the population. And when such are the mores of the community, it would be unwise for a court to bar their expression in the newspapers, books, and magazines of the day."[34]

In a case arising from publication of a photograph of an accident victim's body, a Massachusetts court said: "The law does not provide a remedy for every annoyance that occurs in everyday life. Many things which are distressing or may be lacking in propriety or good taste are not actionable."[35]

Private Information

The facts publicized must be private, not public. The U.S. Supreme Court has held that sanctions may not be imposed for the accurate publication of material from public records or information in the public domain although innocent individuals, through no fault of their own, may suffer embarrassment.[36] Names of crime victims or criminal suspects and embarrassing personal facts introduced into court testimony are examples of information that is not actionable because it comes from public records. The state's rehabilitative interest in protecting identity of juveniles who commit crimes is not sufficient to justify prior restraint.[37] While states may refuse to make public information about juvenile offenders, they may not punish or prohibit media from accurately publishing information learned from other sources.

Personal information that is not a matter of public record but that is known to a large number of people is not considered private, especially if it is used in a newsworthy context. For example, a man who may have saved President Gerald Ford's life in an assassination attempt sued for invasion of privacy after newspapers revealed the fact that he was a homosexual. A court dismissed his argument that his sexual orientation was private information, unknown to members of his family and many of his acquaintances, holding instead that because he had been active in promoting gay rights and in campaigning for the election of homosexual political candidates, his homosexuality was no longer a private fact.[38]

It is important to remember that, unlike in libel suits, truth is not a defense for publishing embarrassing private information that is highly offensive. Therefore, a case can turn on whether highly offensive embarrassing information about a particular person has become a matter of public record. In a story detailing complaints and a state investigation about a county-operated juvenile home, the *Des Moines Register* published the name of a woman who had been involuntarily sterilized at the institution when she was 18 years old. In the lawsuit that followed, the newspaper established that her name had become a matter of public record because it was included in a letter to the state governor, and the governor's correspondence was public record in Iowa. In dismissing the case, the Iowa supreme court said that the story was newsworthy and the use of the specific name added credibility and "contributed constructively to the impact of the article."[39]

The *Oakland Tribune* was unsuccessful, however, in arguing that a birth certificate was a public record. The paper was successfully sued for publication of private information after it revealed that the elected student body president at an area college had undergone a sex change.[40] The plaintiff in that case had taken measures to keep this fact out of the public domain.

In most states that have ruled on the question, once a fact is a matter of public record, it remains public record.[41] Therefore, a time lapse will not defeat the defense. California takes a different approach, allowing juries to determine whether a "social value" exists for publishing information from old public records.

Not of Legitimate Public Concern

Another element in this invasion of privacy tort is that the information concerns private information outside the legitimate concern of the general public; that is, the information is not newsworthy. While no specific definition of newsworthiness exists, the *Restatement* gives this analysis: "In determining what is a matter of legitimate public interest, account must be taken of the customs and conventions of the community; and in the last analysis what is proper becomes a matter of the community mores. The line is to be drawn when the publicity ceases to be the giving of information to which the public is entitled, and becomes a morbid and sensational prying into private lives for its own sake, with which a reasonable member of the public, with decent standards, would say he had no concerns."[42]

As noted in the section immediately above, material contained in public records or from public events is generally considered newsworthy. Information about public officials and public figures that even remotely relates to their public lives has been held of public concern.

False Light

Unlike the three invasion of privacy torts discussed thus far, truth is a defense for publication of information that places someone in a false light. This tort is similar to defamation in that falsity is an integral part of the offense, but the harm is mental anguish rather than damage to reputation.

The *Restatement* defines false light as follows: "One who gives publicity to a matter concerning another that places the other before the public in a false light is subject to liability to the other for invasion of his privacy if (a) the false light in which the other was placed would be highly offensive to a reasonable person and (b) the actor had knowledge of or acted in reckless disregard as to the falsity of the publicized matter and the false light in which the other would be placed."[43]

False light privacy is sometimes further categorized as embellishment, distortion and fictionalization. To embellish an account means to add false material to an otherwise accurate story. Distortion refers to the appearance of factual material in a distorted context that a reasonable person would find offensive, and fictionalization includes references to real people either under their own name or a fictitious name in a work of fiction.

Photographs have been the subject of false light privacy actions involving media defendants. While the general rule applies that people in public view may be photographed and their picture published in a newsworthy context, care must be taken that the picture does not accompany a caption or illustrate a story that places the subject in a false light. As an example, consider a photograph taken of a married couple sitting at a farmer's market booth with their arms about each other. The picture itself presents no legal problems because it was taken in a public place. When used by *Harper's Bazaar* to illustrate the theme "love makes the world go around," the couple was unsuccessful in arguing false light privacy.[44] On the other hand, the couple was awarded damages after the same picture illustrated a *Ladies' Home Journal* article about love and divorce and carried a caption that read "Publicized as glamorous and desirable, 'love at first sight' is a bad risk."[45]

A picture of a 10-year-old who narrowly escaped serious injury when she was knocked to the ground by a passing automobile was not actionable as used the following day in a newspaper account of the accident. However, nearly two years later the *Saturday Evening Post* used the same photograph to illustrate an article titled "They Ask to Be Killed," which discussed careless practices that often lead to accidents. Although the child was not named in the article or photo caption, her family successfully argued false light privacy on the grounds that the article falsely implied that her accident was caused by carelessness.[46]

Knowledge of Falsity or Reckless Disregard

The U. S. Supreme Court heard its first privacy case involving the mass media in the 1967 case of Time, Inc. v. Hill, with a plurality holding that in false light privacy cases, as in defamation cases, public figures must prove that the offending publication was made with knowledge of falsity or reckless disregard for truth.[47] Three justices used the reasoning from the landmark New York Times v. Sullivan libel case that erroneous statement, if innocent or merely negligent, must be protected if the freedoms of expression are to have the breathing space they need to survive.

A federal district court in Tennessee has held that plaintiffs in a false light privacy case must prove actual malice if the published material deals with matters of public interest.[48]

Endnotes

1. Restatement of the Law, 2d, Torts, §652A et seq. (1977).

2. The Tennessee Supreme Court indirectly recognized such a right in a 1956 case when it upheld the dismissal of a privacy claim based on precedents established in other states. In Langford v. Vanderbilt University et al., 199 Tenn 389 at 401, after saying that "assuming the existence of such a common law right of action in Tennessee," the state supreme court noted that courts in other states recognizing a right of privacy agree that it "is properly defined as the right to be let alone; the right of a person to be free from unwarranted publicity."

3. T.C.A. 47-25-1101–1108.

4. T.C.A. 47-25-1103.

5. The criminal sanction was added in a 1989 amendment to the act.

6. T.C.A. 47-25-1105.

7. For example, the Second Circuit, applying New York law, ruled that a property right existed in Presley's name and likeness, and it was descendible to Presley's heirs: Factors, Etc. v. Pro Arts, Inc., 579 F.2d 215 (1978). The Sixth Circuit, applying Tennessee law at the time, held that the right to privacy became part of the public domain after an individual's death and thus the Presley estate had no legal authority to control the use of his name or likeness: Memphis Development Foundation v. Factors Etc. Inc., 616 F.2d 956 (1980).

8. In addition to Tennessee, California, Florida, Georgia, Nebraska, Oklahoma, Utah and Virginia had such statutes. In addition, New York law had been interpreted to be descendible.

9. T.C.A. 47-25-1104.

10. T.C.A. 47-25-1107.

11. Namath v. Sports Illustrated, 371 N.Y.S.2d 10 (1975), affirmed, 39 N.Y.S. 2d 897 (1976).

12. Zacchini v. Scripps Howard Broadcasting Co., 433 U.S. 562 (1977).

13. See e.g. Allen v. Men's World Outlet, 679 F.Supp. 360 (1988); Onassis v. Christian Dior, 472 N.Y.S.2d 254 (1984); Midler v. Ford Motor Co., 849 F.2d 460 (9th Cir. 1988) (applying California law).

14. Russell v. Marboro Books, 183 N.Y.S. 2d 8 (1959).

15. Martin v. Senators, Inc., et al., 220 Tenn. 465 (1967).

16. Restatement (2d) of Torts, §652B (1977).

17. Jaubert v. Crowley Post-Signal, Inc., 375 So.2d 1386 (La. 1979).

18. Cefalu v. Globe Newspaper, 391 N.E.2d 935 (1979).

19. Cape Publications, Inc. v. Bridges, 423 So.2d 426 (Fla. App. 1982).

20. Langford v. Vanderbilt University, 199 Tenn. 389.

21. California v. Greenwood, 486 U.S. 35 (1988).

22. Cassidy v. ABC, 60 Ill. App. 3d 831, 377 N.E. 2d 126 (1978).

23. Galella v. Onassis, 487 F.2d 986 (1973); 533 F.Supp. 1076 (1982).

24. Dietemann v. Time, Inc., 449 F.2d at 249 (9th Cir. 1971).

25. Le Mistral, Inc. v. CBS, 402 N.Y.S.2d 815 (1978).

26. Dietemann v. Time, Inc., 449 F.2d at 249 (9th Cir. 1971).

27. Florida v. Fletcher, 340 So.2d 914 (Fla. 1976).

28. Anderson v. WROC-TV, 441 N.Y.S. 220 (1981). See also, Miller v. NBC, 187 Cal. App. 3d 1463.

29. Oklahoma v. Bernstein, 5 Media Law Rptr. 2313 (1980, affirmed Stahl v. State, 665 P.2d 839, 9 Media Law Rptr. 1945 (Okla. Crim. 1983), cert. denied, 464 U.S. 1069 (1984).

30. Restatement (2d) of Torts, §652D (1977).

31. Porten v. University of San Francisco, 64 Cal. App3d 825 (1976).

32. Hendry v. Conner, 226 N.W.2d 921 (1975).

33. Henderson v. Ripperger, 3 Kan. App. 2d 303, 594 P.2d 251 (1979).

34. Sidis v. F-R Publishing Corp., 113 F.2d 806 (2nd Cir.), cert. denied, 311 U.S. 711 (1940).

35. Kelley v. Post Pub. Co., 989 N.E.2d 285 (1951).

36. See e.g., Cox Broadcasting Corp. v. Cohn, 420 U.S. 469 (1975); Florida Star v. B.J.F., 491 U.S. 524 (1989).

37. Smith v. Daily Mail Publishing Co., 443 U.S. 97 (1979).

38. Sipple v. Chronicle Publishing, 154 Cal. App.3d 1040 (1984).

39. Howard v. Des Moines Register, 283 N.W.2d 289, cert. denied 445 U.S. 904 (1980).

40. Diaz v. Oakland Tribune, 139 Cal. App.3d 118 (1983).

41. Where, as in Tennessee, certain classes of crimes can be expunged from the record, the statute of limitations usually allows a shorter time for filing a privacy action than for petitioning to have records expunged.

42. Restatement (2d) of Torts, §652D (1977).

43. Restatement (2d) of Torts, §652E (1977).

44. Gill v. Hearst Pub. Co., 253 P.2d 441 (1953).

45. Gill v. Curtis Pub. Co., 239 P.2d 630 (1952).

46. Leaverton v. Curtis Pub. Co., 192 F.2d (3rd Cir. 1951).

47. Time, Inc. v. Hill, 385 U.S. 374 (1967).

48. Roberts v. Dover, 525 F. Supp. 987 (M.D. Tenn. 1981).

Advertising

For most of our nation's history, advertising, also referred to as "commercial speech," was outside the protective umbrella of the First Amendment, meaning that messages written or spoken to promote goods and services could be censored or prohibited. During the 1970s, the U. S. Supreme Court began to afford advertising some First Amendment protection.

Regulation of Advertising

All levels of government, as well as trade and professional associations, mass media, and individual advertisers, have assumed roles in regulating advertising. Self-regulation by the media, by advertisers and by trade and professional associations attempts to gain public trust and credibility and to head off increased governmental regulation. This chapter will focus on regulation of commercial speech that comes from governmental entities, with emphasis on Tennessee laws and regulations affecting advertising.

Extent of First Amendment Protection

Communications law governing editorial copy–for example, the law of libel, privacy, and copyright–applies also to advertising copy. In addition, the Supreme Court has held that commercial speech does not warrant as much freedom under the First Amendment as noncommercial speech receives. Although in most contexts it would be an unconstitutional prior restraint for the government to prohibit or to punish words on the basis that they are false or misleading, government has such power where the words are used in advertisements.

During the 1970s the U.S. Supreme Court began to declare that some state prohibitions on advertising were an unconstitutional infringement on the public's right to receive information about products or services. The "right to know" reasoning opened the way to advertise abortion services,[1] prices of prescription drugs,[2] eyeglasses,[3] and attorneys' services.[4]

In a 1980 case,[5] the Supreme Court set forth a four-part test for judging the extent to which advertising could be prohibited or regulated. The court said advertising has no First Amendment protection and can be prohibited if it

- promotes an illegal product or service, or
- is false or misleading.

If the advertising message is neither false or misleading and promotes a legal product or service, the Supreme Court said the government could still regulate the message, provided that the regulation

- is justified by a substantial government interest, and
- directly advances the governmental interest in a manner no more extensive than necessary to accomplish that interest.

In the case resulting in that ruling, the advertising being prohibited by the state of New York was promotional advertising for an electric utility company. The product or service was legal, and the advertising was truthful and not misleading. Therefore, it passed the first two parts of the four-part test and was eligible for First Amendment protection.

The governmental interest being served by the prohibition was energy conservation, certainly a valid, substantial interest during the nationwide energy crisis at that time. However, the Supreme Court held that the state's ban failed the fourth part of the test because it was more extensive than necessary. The court thought that energy conservation could have been furthered in some way less restrictive than a total ban on the utility company's promotional advertising.

In at least two cases since 1980, a Supreme Court majority has allowed advertising restrictions to stand even though they were not the least restrictive means of accomplishing the asserted valid governmental interest. In those cases, the court held that so long as the government's restrictions were "reasonable" means of accomplishing the asserted interest, they were constitutional.[6]

Right to Refuse Advertising

Many mass media outlets, although highly dependent on advertising revenue, nevertheless impose restrictions on advertising they will publish. For example, because of personal principles or the fear of alienating audiences, many print and broadcast media will not accept advertising for products such as X-rated movies, alcohol, and tobacco or services such as massage parlors and fortune telling. Advertising rate cards often list types of advertising copy or art that publishers will not accept.

As a general rule, mass media—both print and broad—castare privately owned businesses and have the legal right to refuse service to whomever they choose. This right has been upheld by both federal and state courts.[7] Exceptions to this general rule fall into three areas:

- contract violations,
- use of broadcasting facilities by candidates for elective federal offices, and
- violations of anti-trust laws.

It is important for sales personnel to know company policy about unacceptable advertising because if a contractual agreement is entered into, that agreement can be legally enforced. For example, in a situation where a newspaper had a contract to publish a political candidate's ad, a court held that it would be a contract violation to refuse to publish the ad.[8] The newspaper wanted to back out on the deal because the copy for the advertising was considered "inflammatory."

The narrow exemption for broadcasters to the general right to refuse advertising is for candidates for federal office during an election campaign. Congress, in its own self-interest, legislated that the FCC has the power to revoke a station license "for willful or repeated failure to allow reasonable access to or to permit purchase of reasonable amounts of time for the use of a broadcasting station by a legally qualified candidate for federal elective office on behalf of his candidacy." [9]

Broadcasters are not obligated to sell advertising time to candidates for state or local offices. A broadcaster who chooses to do so, however, must allow all candidates for that same office an equal opportunity to buy advertising time.[10]

The mass media, like other business, are subject to federal antitrust laws designed to promote competition. The First Amendment does not provide a shield for the media from anti-competitive activities.[11] Court rulings have gone against the media where a newspaper refused to sell advertising to firms that also advertised with a local radio station[12] and a newspaper that refused to sell advertising space unless buyers purchased space in the morning, afternoon and Sunday editions.[13]

Federal Regulation

The Federal Trade Commission is chief among many federal agencies with regulatory power over advertising. Others include the Food and Drug Administration, the Federal Communications Commission, the postal service, and the Securities and Exchange Commission.

Congress has given the FTC the authority to take action against advertising affecting interstate commerce that is false or deceptive. No definition of "false or deceptive" is given, and because commissioners are appointed by the president and confirmed by the Senate, the FTC's aggressiveness varies somewhat with the political climate in Washington.

Whether representations in advertising are untrue, deceptive, or misleading is a question of fact depending on the circumstances of the particular case.[14] The commission generally judges advertising according to whether reasonable consumers are likely to be mislead in a material way because of a representation, omission or practice used in promoting goods or services. The section that follows briefly describes or gives examples of these considerations.

The FTC generally will not act unless "material" representations, omissions, or practices are involved. By "material" the FTC means those that are likely to influence consumers to either buy or not buy something. Some kinds of information are more influential than others in buying decisions. The FTC has considered statements about safety and health, costs, durability, performance, and quality, among others, to be material. For example, where a spokesman for a gasoline additive falsely claimed to be standing in front of a research laboratory, an administrative law judge held that such a statement was not influential in purchasing decisions. What the spokesman said about the product, not the location for his pitch, was material.

Mock-ups for television have been held deceptive and material when they were used to support specific claims for a product, as where the claim was made that a shaving cream was effective enough to shave sandpaper, and presumably, tough beards. Instead of sandpaper, however, glass with sand sprinkled on it was used in the television commercial. On the other hand, the use of mashed potatoes to represent ice cream under hot television studio lights would not be material and deceptive so long as no claim was made that would be supported by the substitution, such as how fast a particular ice cream brand melted.

Advertising statements may be literally true but still mislead consumers if they omit important information or use language that is commonly misunderstood. For example, an ad saying that a finance company would give customers "instant tax refunds" was held misleading because it did not make clear that customers had to qualify for a loan first, a procedure that was somewhat time consuming. Statements about the efficacy of a health aid is misleading if they fail to make clear that the product is not safe for people with certain medical conditions. Wonder Bread's claim to be fortified with vitamins and minerals was considered misleading because it did not make clear that nearly all commercially baked bread had the same characteristics.

The audience for the which the advertising is directed is another FTC consideration in determining whether an ad is false or misleading. The "reasonable" person, rather than the most gullible person, within the audience is the test. The FTC may determine that advertising containing technical language misleads a lay audience, but the same ad might be acceptable for a specialized audience, such as physicians, auto mechanics, or lawyers. The same idea applies for ads directed toward children. For example, special effects should not be used for demonstrating toys on television in ways that deceive children into believing that the toy "goes faster," is larger, more colorful and so forth than it actually is.

Safety considerations unrelated to advertising claims are considered in deciding whether action should be taken against a particular advertisement. For example, the FTC may seek to stop print or broadcast ads showing electrical appliances being used near a swimming pool or the practice of distributing free samples of a product like razor blades inside a rolled up newspaper thrown on the doorstep.

The FTC will accept a rather large amount of "puffery"–exaggerated claims for a product–when reasonable people among the intended audience are not likely to take such claims seriously. Examples of such puffery often fall into subjective categories that something feels, tastes, smells, or looks "best."

If an advertiser makes a claim that can be objectively substantiated, the FTC may ask the advertiser to document that claim. For example, an advertiser should be prepared to give scientific proof for the claim that a product "will operate effectively for ten years" or that "more doctors use" this product than use its competitor.

Testimonials for a product must meet specific guidelines. The person giving the testimonial must actually use the product and must be qualified to judge its quality; therefore, ads showing a professional basketball player endorsing a technical product for which he has no expertise are questionable.

Merchants must take care in listing prices in advertisements so as to avoid misleading or deceiving consumers. "Bait and switch" tactics are illegally deceptive. These involve advertising a product at a cheap price to lure consumers into a store and then using high-pressure sales tactics to persuade customers to buy a more expensive model. "Loss-leader" advertising is not illegal in most states. This is the practice of advertising an item or several items at below cost in order to entice customers into the store, where they are likely to purchase additional items at regular costs.

Advertisements should not say a product is being sold at a "reduced," "discounted," or "special introductory" price unless that is true. If customers must purchase an additional item in order to get something "free," the advertisement must clearly state that fact, and the price of the additional item must not be inflated to cover the free item.

Advertising Regulation in Tennessee

The Tennessee Supreme Court has held that commercial speech enjoys a qualified protection under the First Amendment and under Article I, Section 19 of the Tennessee Constitution.[15] Advertising in Tennessee may be regulated as to time, place, and manner, provided that the restrictions:

- are justified without reference to the content;
- serve a significant governmental interest;
- leave open ample alternative channels of communication.[16]

Advertising as Deceptive Business Practice

A person who "with intent to deceive . . . makes a false or misleading statement in any advertisements addressed to the public or to a substantial segment thereof for the purposes of promoting the purchase or sale of property or services" is guilty of a deceptive business practice, which is a Class B misdemeanor under Tennessee law.[17] This particular statute does not define "false" or "misleading," and other state statutes regulating practices within certain industries also lack definitions of these terms, but they do specify advertising practices that will be considered false or misleading or both.

Statutes Regulating Ads for Specific Products and Industries

Food, Drugs and Cosmetics

Tennessee law states that an ad for a drug or device is false if it conveys to the general public rather than to members of the medical, dental, pharmaceutical or veterinary professions that the product will have any effect upon a large listing of diseases and disorders, including appendicitis, blood poison, cancer, diabetes, heart and vascular diseases, high blood pressure, tuberculosis and sexual impotence.[18]

Insurance

The section of the statute defining unfair or deceptive acts or practices within the insurance business includes "untrue, deceptive, misleading" advertising among the list of prohibited misrepresentative statements about insurance policies.[19]

Employment

A statute dealing with procuring employees makes it unlawful to use false advertising "concerning the kind and character of the work to be done, or amount and character of the compensation to be paid for such work, or the sanitary or other conditions of the employment, or as to the existence or nonexistence of a strike, or other trouble pending between employer and employees."[20] The General Assembly included in the statute its intent that the law be construed as applying only in cases where workers are brought into the state or induced to go from one place in the state to another.[21]

Time-Share Property

Two statutes passed in 1983 deal with advertising and promotional offers for time-share property. Thirteen specific prohibitions are listed concerning advertising for time shares[22] and an equal number of acts or practices are declared unfair in connection with promotional offers for such property.[23] A 1990 law[24] makes time-share resale brokers subject to the same provisions of the 1983 statutes and further specifies that advertising seeking to sell the services of time-share resale brokers must include a disclaimer that "there is no guarantee that your time-share interval can be sold at any particular price or within any particular period of time."[25]

Mortgage Loans

Advertising pertaining to mortgage loans or the availability of such loans must not be false or misleading "with the intention to defraud the public."[26]

Rentals

In Tennessee it is unlawful for rental location agents to publish advertising without their names and the fact that they are rental location agents.[27]

Another statute lists specific information that must be included in an advertisement for a rental-purchase agreement if the ad refers to or states the amount of any payment or refers to the right to acquire ownership for any specific item.[28]

Alcoholic Beverages

Only one outdoor sign is permitted at retail beer establishments, and while the sign may state that the store sells beer, it may not use "brand names, pictures, numbers, prices or diagrams relating to beer."[29]

Tobacco

Retailers are prohibited from advertising any cigarettes for less than cost, and from including cigarettes in combination sales whereby cigarettes are combined with another product and sold at a price that is less than the aggregate of the prices for the items sold separately.[30]

Dairy Products

Among the rules concerning advertising dairy products is one that prohibits retailers from advertising any milk product for less than cost, and another that makes it illegal to include milk products in combination sales whereby a milk product is combined with another product and sold at a price that is less than the aggregate of the prices for the items sold separately.[31]

A Tennessee court case has held that trading stamps can not be given for milk purchases unless the milk is priced at more than the invoice minimum plus eight percent.[32]

Demonstrating a concern that the public will be misled or deceived about dairy "trade products," meaning dairy substitutes, the statutes specify that no picture or representation of a bovine or any symbol or term commonly associated with dairy farming may be used in ads for trade products. Before being used, labels and packaging must be registered with the commissioner of agriculture.[33]

Meat and Meat Products

False or misleading advertising is prohibited, as are "bait and switch" tactics. It is also illegal for any advertising medium to knowingly publish such advertising regarding meat or poultry products.[34]

Other Products and Services

Tennessee statutes specifically prohibit false and misleading advertising and certain practices in advertising agricultural and vegetable seeds,[35] hotels, inns and other transient lodging places,[36] industrial loan and thrift companies,[37] abandoned property in self-service storage facilities,[38] and the sale, advertising and distribution of coupons.[39]

Advertising by Licensed Professionals

In addition to the general prohibition against deceptive business practices, other state statutes and judicial rules determine how people in specific professions may advertising in Tennessee. False or misleading advertising is often grounds for suspending or revoking a professional's license to practice in the state. This section summarizes some of the regulations governing advertising by professionals in Tennessee.

Attorneys

The state supreme court, in its code of professional responsibility for attorneys,[40] has promulgated rules regarding publicity.[41] False, fraudulent, misleading or deceptive statements or claims are prohibited. A statement or claim is defined as false, fraudulent, misleading or deceptive if it:

- "contains a material misrepresentation of fact or law, or omits a fact necessary to make the statement, considered as a whole, not materially misleading;
- "is likely to create an unjustified expectation about results the lawyer can achieve, or states or implies that the lawyer can achieve results by means that violate the disciplinary rules or other law; or
- "compares the lawyer's services with other lawyers' services, unless the comparison can be factually substantiated."[42]

The code specifies that lawyers must limit their advertising to "established" print or broadcast media in the geographical area in which they reside or maintain offices. Handbills, circulars or similar material must be delivered by someone other than the attorney or firm being advertised. In addition, twenty-five paragraphs in the code of professional responsibility delineate types of information that lawyers may include in advertising materials.

Any printed or broadcast material soliciting professional employment from a prospective client known to be in the need of legal services in a particular matter must include the words "this is an advertisement." Further, the code specifies the type size, duration for broadcast, and placement of the notice.[43]

Within three days after an ad has been published, a copy must be filed with the Board of Professional Responsibility. Sanctions for violating the code include disciplinary action and an injunction to restrain further publication of the advertisement.

If an attorney advertises a fee for a legal service, the ad is evidence of the reasonableness of the fee, and a court must not award a fee in excess of the advertised amount without proof that additional compensation is warranted.[44]

Healing Arts

The licensing boards of the respective branches of the healing arts are authorized to make rules and regulations to regulate the nature, manner, content, and extent of advertising by practitioners under their jurisdiction.[45]

The "use of untruthful or misleading statements, or exaggerated or extravagant claims concerning [a licensee's] professional excellence or abilities" is grounds for suspension or revocation of the license of practitioners of the healing arts.[46] Practitioners must not use advertising "tending to deceive or mislead the public,"[47] promoting a "system or mode of healing" for which one is not licensed[48] or offering free professional services or examinations.[49]

Still other statutes prohibit misleading and false advertising for healing arts practitioners such as chiropractors,[50] dentists,[51] opticians,[52] optometrists,[53] osteopathic physicians,[54] pharmacists,[55] physicians and surgeons,[56] podiatrists,[57] respiratory care practitioners,[58] counselors and marital and family therapists.[59] In some instances, sanctions, including civil penalties, are specified in addition to the potential of having a license suspended or revoked.

Pharmacists must not advertise prescriptions at any location other than at a licensed pharmacy.[60]

Funeral directors and embalmers

Misleading or false advertising is grounds for refusal, suspension or revocation of a license.[61]

Political Campaigns

Advertisements for candidates for public office must carry the name of the sponsor, and if sponsored by an organization, committee, or association, must give the names of the principal officers.[62] In Tennessee it is a misdemeanor to publish or distribute campaign literature opposing a candidate with the knowledge that it contains false information.[63]

It is also a misdemeanor with a mandatory minimum sentence of 48 hours in jail to publish, distribute or transport campaign literature that endorses a candidate with the intent to misrepresent the identity of an organization or person making the endorsement.[64]

It is against Tennessee law to attach campaign advertising to any kind of pole, tower or fixture of a public utility company without legal authority within any county with a metropolitan form of government, as well as other counties falling within specified population ranges.[65]

Campaign signs, posters, or placards for candidates on highway rights-of-way or other publicly owned property must be removed within three weeks after an election. A candidate in a primary election who becomes a candidate in a special or general election may leave signs in place until three weeks after the general or special election.[66] Violations of the statute carry no penalty, however.

In 1992, a divided U.S. Supreme Court upheld a Tennessee law banning campaign literature or the solicitation of votes within 100 feet of the entrances to polling places.[67] The state supreme court had ruled the statute[68] unconstitutional on the grounds that it was not narrowly tailored to protect the state's interest in preventing voter intimidation and election fraud and was not the least restrictive means of protecting that interest.[69]

In reversing and remanding the case, a plurality[70] of the U.S. Supreme Court determined that the statute survived strict scrutiny. In attempting to balance the conflict between two fundamental rights the exercise of free speech and right to vote without intimidation or fraud the state's compromise with the 100-foot campaign-free zone was sufficiently narrow to be constitutional, the court ruled.

Telemarketing and Use of Fax Machines

Responding to complaints about telephone service being tied up by unsolicited, recorded advertising messages, the Tennessee General Assembly passed the Consumer Telemarketing Protection Act of 1990.[71] The statute makes it unlawful to use equipment that automatically selects and dials telephone numbers and disseminates recorded messages for advertising or selling purposes or for conducting polls or soliciting information unless these conditions are met:

- prior written consent has been received or an operator introduces the call and receives consent;
- calls are made between 8 a.m. and 9 p.m.;
- calls must terminate within ten seconds after a person answering either hangs up or fails to give consent to play a recorded message.

Public schools, kindergarten through high school, are exempt if the calls are part of a program to regulate and control student absenteeism.[72]

A 1990 statute also made it illegal to initiate unsolicited telefax messages promoting goods or services.[73]

The Tennessee Supreme Court struck down as violations of both the federal and state constitutions a statute[74] that prohibited telephone solicitations by professional solicitors and that established a percentage-based regulation upon the fees that could be collected by professional solicitors.[75] The statute has been repealed.

State Taxes on Advertising

Periodicals printed entirely on newsprint or bond paper and regularly distributed on a weekly or more frequent basis, and advertising supplements or other printed matter distributed with such periodicals are exempt from Tennessee sales taxes.[76] A multi-page advertising circular devoid of local news was not a newspaper and did not qualify for exemption, the Tennessee Supreme Court held.[77]

Also exempt, by a 1991 amendment, are "magazines and books which are distributed and sold to consumers by United States mail or common carrier, where the only activities of the seller or distributor in Tennessee are those activities having to do with the printing, storage, labeling and/or delivery to the United States mail or common carrier of such magazines or books, or the maintenance of raw materials with respect to such activities, notwithstanding that such seller or distributor maintains in Tennessee employees solely in connection with the production and quality control of such printing, storage, labeling and/or delivery, or in connection with news gathering and reporting."[78]

Before the statute was amended in 1991 to include magazines, it exempted only newspapers and accompanying advertising materials. *Newsweek* magazine challenged the statute on the basis that it discriminated against magazines. The Tennessee Supreme Court agreed, holding that to subject magazines and not newspapers to the sales tax on magazines was invalid under the First Amendment.[79] The state argued that newspapers rather than magazines qualified for the tax exemption because they "delivered news and information in a timely and immediate manner,"[80] which seems to ignore that weekly newsmagazines are published as frequently as weekly newspapers in the state. The court was unpersuaded that the argument provided compelling justification for such selective, content-based taxation.

Cooperative direct mail advertising is exempt from state sales taxes if it is distributed within Tennessee from outside the state by a person engaged solely and exclusively in the business of coop direct mail advertising. The statute defines this type of advertising as advertising in the form of discount coupons or leaflets for more than one business that are delivered by mail in a single package to potential customers.[81]

Cable television is not exempt from state sales taxes in Tennessee. Based on the U.S. Supreme Court's 1991 decision in a challenge to an Arkansas statute, such a media-based exemption is valid.[82]

Legal Notice for Court-Ordered Sales

Legal notice must be given at least three different times for court-ordered foreclosure sales valued at more than $200. The notice should appear in a newspaper published in the county where the sale is to be made, with the first publication at least 20 days before the sale.[83]

If no newspaper is published within the county where the sale is to take place, newspaper advertising is dispensed with unless ordered by a court;[84] however, another state statute specifies that when a foreclosure notice cannot be made by newspaper, written notices must be posted for 30 days in at least five of the most public places in the county, one of which must be the courthouse door and another in the neighborhood of the defendant. In addition, if the sale involves real estate, notice must be posted in the civil district where the land lies.[85]

Decisions by Tennessee courts are mixed on whether the failure to give notice affects the validity of the sale. Two appellate court decisions have held that the foreclosure of a trust deed[86] or land sale[87] could be set aside if statutory notice provisions were not followed properly. However, decisions as early as 1872[88] and as late as 1941[89] held that a failure to comply with notice statutes do not render a sale void. A statute provides that a sale made without notice "shall not, on that account, be either void or voidable,"[90] but an officer who fails to comply with the notice provisions is guilty of a Class C misdemeanor and is liable to the party injured for all damages resulting from the failure.[91]

In Tennessee, a newspaper may not charge or receive more than its regular classified advertising rate for publishing legal notices.[92]

Media Liability

Several Tennessee statutes detailing prohibited advertising practices within an industry specifically exempt the media and media employees from any liability for false, deceptive or misleading advertising.[93]

In some instances, media personnel may be held liable if they refuse to cooperate in efforts to identify and locate those placing illegal advertisements[94] or have knowledge of an ad's falsity.[95]

Endnotes

1. Bigelow v. Virginia, 421 U.S. 809, 95 S.Ct. 2222 (1975).

2. Virginia State Board of Pharmacy v. Virginia Citizens Consumer Council, Inc., 425 U.S. 748, 96 S.Ct. 1817 (1976).

3. Horner-Rausch Optical Co. v. Ashley, 547 S.W.2d 577 (Tenn. App. 1976).

4. Bates v. State Bar of Arizona, 433 U.S. 350, 97 S.Ct. 2691 (1977).

5. Central Hudson Gas & Electric Corp. v. Public Service Commission of New York, 447 U.S. 557, 100 S.Ct. 2343.

6. See Posadas de Puerto Rico v. Tourism Co. of Puerto Rico, 478 U.S. 328, 106 S.Ct. 2966 (1986) and Board of Trustees, S.U.N.Y. v. Fox, 109 S.Ct. 3028 (1989).

7. See for example, CBS, Inc. v. Democratic National Committee, 412 U.S. 94 (1973) and Newspaper Printing Corp. v. Galbreath, 580 S.W.2d 777 (Tenn. 1979), cert. denied, 444 U.S. 870 (1979).

8. Herald Telephone v. Fatouros, 431 N.E.2d 171 (Ind. App. 4th Dist. 1982), 8 Media Law Rptr. 1230.

9. Communications Act of 1934, as amended 47 U.S.C.A. 312.

10. Id., § 315.

11. Associated Press v. U.S. 326 U.S. 1 (1945).

12. Lorain Journal Co. v. U.S., 342 U.S. 143 (1951).

13. Kansas City Star Co. v. U.S. 240 F.2d 643 (8th Cir.), cert. denied 354 U.S. 923 (1957).

14. 32 Am Jur 2d §99, citing People v. Byrnes, 190 P2d 584 and People v. Charles E. Austin, Inc. 3 NW2d 841.

15. H & L Messengers, Inc. v. City of Brentwood, 577 S.W.2d 444 (Tenn. 1979).

16. Id.

17. T.C.A. 39-14-127(5).

18. T.C.A. 53-1-113.

19. T.C.A. 56-8-104(1).

20. T.C.A. 50-1-102(a)(1).

21. T.C.A. 50-1-102(e).

22. T.C.A. 66-32-131.

23. T.C.A. 66-32-133.

24. T.C.A. 66-32-136.

25. T.C.A. 66-32-136(c).

26. T.C.A. 45-13-115.

27. T.C.A. 62-25-105.

28. T.C.A. 47-18-610.

29. T.C.A. 57-5-304.

30. T.C.A. 47-25-310.

31. T.C.A. 53-3-202(b)(1).

32. Hogue v. Kroger Co., 213 Tenn. 365 (1963).

33. T.C.A. 53-3-107.

34. T.C.A. 53-7-206(5)

35. T.C.A. 43-10-109.

36. T.C.A. 67-4-1407.

37. T.C.A. 45-5-303.

38. T.C.A. 66-31-105.

39. T.C.A. 47-25-808.

40. Rule 8, Canon 2, Rules of the Supreme Court.

41. Rule 8, Disciplinary Rule 2-101, Tennessee Court Rules Annotated.

42. Id., Disciplinary Rule 2-101(A).

43. Id., Disciplinary Rule 2-101(N).

44. T.C.A. 23-3-109.

45. T.C.A. 63-1-116..

46. T.C.A. 63-1-102.

47. T.C.A. 63-1-120(16).

48. T.C.A. 63-1-120(13).

49. T.C.A. 63-1-120(17).

50. T.C.A. 63-4-114(13) and (16).

51. T.C.A. 63-5-124

52. T.C.A. 63-14-103.

53. T.C.A. 63-8-113.

54. T.C.A. 63-9-111.

55. T.C.A. 63-10-207.

56. T.C.A. 63-6-214.

57. T.C.A. 63-3-119.

58. T.C.A. 63-6-411.

59. T.C.A. 63-22-115.

60. T.C.A. 63-10-207.

61. T.C.A. 62-5-317.

62. T.C.A. 2-19-120.

63. T.C.A. 2-19-142.

64. T.C.A. 2-19-116.

65. T.C.A. 2-19-144.

66. T.C.A. 2-1-116.

67. Burson v. Freeman, 1992 WESTLAW 107344, 20 Med. L. Rptr. 1137.

68. T.C.A. 2-7-111(b). The statute was amended to extend the ban to 300 feet in 12 counties, according to population.

69. Freeman v. Burson, 802 S.W.2d 210 (Tenn. 1990), reversed by U.S. Supreme Court, 1992 WESTLAW 107344, 20 Med. L. Rptr. 1137 (1992).

70. Justices Blackmun, White, Kennedy and Chief Justice Rehnquist. Justice Scalia concurred in the judgment but disagreed with the public forum and strict scrutiny analysis.

71. T.C.A. 47-18-1502.

72. T.C.A. 47-18-1507.

73. T.C.A. 47-18-1602.

74. T.C.A. 48-3-513 (repealed).

75. WRG Enterprises, Inc. v. Crowell, 758 S.W.2d 214 (1988).

76. T.C.A. 67-6-329(25).

77. Shoppers Guide Publishing Co. v. Woods, 547 S.W.2d 561 (Tenn. 1977); Memphis Shoppers News, Inc. v. Woods, 584 S.W.2d 196 (Tenn. 1979).

78. T.C.A. 67-6-329(20).

79. Newsweek, Inc. v. Celauro, 789 S.W.2d 247 (Tenn. 1990).

80. Id. at 250.

81. T.C.A. 67-6-344.

82. Leathers v. Medlock, 113 L.Ed.2d 494.

83. T.C.A. 35-5-101.

84. T.C.A. 35-5-102.

85. T.C.A. 35-5-103.

86. Clack v. Standefer, 24 Tenn. App. 556, 147 S.W.2d 764 (1940).

87. Napier v. Stone, 21 Tenn. App. 626, 114 S.W.2d 57 (1937).

88. Howell v. Donaldson, 54 Tenn. 206; Childress v. Harrison, 60 Tenn. 410; Downing v. Stephens, 60 Tenn. 454.

89. Williams v. Williams, 25 Tenn. App. 290, 156 S.W.2d 363.

90. T.C.A. 35-5-106.

91. T.C.A. 35-5-107.

92. T.C.A. 8-21-1301.

93. See, for example, T.C.A. 66-32-131, 45-13-115, and 53-1-103(c).

94. T.C.A. 53-1-103(c).

95. T.C.A. 66-32-131.

Obscenity

Obscenity is a category of expression outside the protection of either the federal or state constitution[1] Thus, the state may regulate and prohibit the distribution of obscene material so long as the legislation does not infringe upon recognized constitutional rights, is not unconstitutionally vague, and does not violate the equal protection or due process of the law.[2]

The major problem in governmental efforts to eliminate obscenity and to prosecute those who manufacture or distribute obscene material is a definitional problem–where to draw the line between sexually explicit material that is constitutionally protected expression and that which is not. As the U.S. Supreme Court has noted,[3] pornographic material is not necessarily obscene. Obscenity has a specific judicial meaning.

Tennessee Obscenity Statutes

Tennessee obscenity statutes[4] were rewritten as part of the revised criminal code, effective on Nov. 1, 1989. The former laws, as amended, had withstood many constitutional challenges.[5]

Tennessee law makes it a Class A misdemeanor[6] "to knowingly produce, send or cause to be sent, or bring or cause to be brought, into this state for sale, distribution, exhibition or display, or in this state to prepare for distribution, publish, print, exhibit, distribute, or offer to distribute, or to possess with intent to distribute or to exhibit or offer to distribute any obscene matter."[7] Further, "it is unlawful to direct, present or produce any obscene theatrical production, peep show or live performance, and every person who participates in that part of such production which renders the production or performance obscene is guilty of the offense."[8]

The statute exempts persons possessing obscene material for scientific, educational, governmental or other similar justification.[9]

Definition of Obscenity

In defining obscenity, Tennessee law draws from the United States Supreme Court's three-part test in a 1973 case.[10] The state statute states that "obscene" means:[11]

(A) The average person applying contemporary community standards would find that the work, taken as a whole, appeals to the prurient interest;

(B) The average person applying contemporary community standards would find that the work depicts or describes, in a patently offensive way, sexual conduct; and

(C) The work, taken as a whole, lacks serious literary, artistic, political, or scientific value.

The U.S. Supreme Court has held that material designed to appeal to the prurient interests of audiences other than "average persons" is punishable if "the dominant theme of the material taken as a whole appeals to the prurient interests of the members of that group."[12] A Tennessee court ruled that the accused had the burden of proof to establish that the matter was designed for or primarily disseminated to a particular sexually deviant group before the state was not required to establish that material appealed to the prurient interest of that particular group.[13]

Community

In 1990 the Tennessee General Assembly changed the scope of the "community" from the entire state to the judicial district in which a violation of the obscenity statute is alleged to have occurred.[14] The state of Tennessee is divided into 31 separate judicial districts. (See section on Courts in Tennessee in this book for counties within each judicial district.)

The Tennessee Court of Criminal Appeals has held that the state is not required to present evidence of contemporary community standards or expert testimony that the acts complained of were obscene. Rather, the jurors may determine whether conduct is obscene from their own knowledge of the community.[15]

Patently Offensive Sexual Conduct

"Patently offensive," as defined by Tennessee statute[16] means "that which goes substantially beyond customary limits of candor in describing or representing such matters." "Prurient interest" means a shameful or morbid interest in sex.[17]

The section of the Tennessee statute defining "sexual conduct"[18] reads as follows:

(A) "Patently offensive representations or descriptions of ultimate sexual acts, normal or perverted, actual or simulated. A sexual act is simulated when it depicts explicit sexual activity which gives the appearance of ultimate sexual acts, anal, oral or genital. 'Ultimate sexual acts' means sexual intercourse, anal or otherwise, fellatio, cunnilingus or sodomy; or

(B) "Patently offensive representations or descriptions of masturbation, excretory functions, and lewd exhibition of the genitals."

Knowledge of Obscenity

Tennessee law specified that a person is deemed to have "actual or constructive knowledge" of the contents of material who has knowledge of facts that "would put a reasonable and prudent person on notice as to the suspect nature of the material."[19]

The Tennessee Court of Criminal Appeals refused a defendant's argument that he did not know the material was obscene. The court noted in that case that the defendant owned nearly all of the establishment selling the material, received most of the profit, ordered and unpacked most of the merchandise to be sold.[20]

Statutes Protecting Minors

Tennessee law makes it unlawful to hire, employ or use minors, defined as those under eighteen years of age, in the production, distribution, exhibition or display of obscene material.[21] Violation of this subsection of the statute is a Class E felony plus a fine of from $10,000 to $100,000.[22]

It is also a crime in Tennessee, punishable as a Class A misdemeanor, to knowingly sell or loan for monetary consideration or otherwise exhibit to minors material "which depicts nudity, sexual conduct, excess violence, or sadomasochistic abuse, and which is harmful to minors" unless the minor is accompanied by his or her parent or legal guardian or by an adult with the written permission of the parent or legal guardian.[23]

The statute defines "harmful to minors" as "that quality of any description or representation, in whatever form, of nudity, sexual excitement, sexual conduct, excess violence or sadomasochistic abuse when the matter or performance:[24]

(A) "Would be found by the average person applying contemporary community standards to appeal predominantly to the prurient, shameful or morbid interests of minors;

(B) "Is patently offensive to prevailing standards in the adult community as a whole with respect to what is suitable for minors; and

(C) "Taken as whole lacks serious literary, artistic, political or scientific values for minors."

"Excess violence" is defined as "the depiction of acts of violence in such a graphic and/or bloody manner as to exceed common limits of custom and candor, or in such a manner that it is apparent that the predominant appeal of the material is portrayal of violence for violence's sake."[25] There have been no reported cases of prosecutions under this statute, which became effective Nov. 1, 1989.

Another Tennessee statute makes it unlawful "to display for sale or rental a visual depiction, including a videocassette tape or film, or a written representation, including a book, magazine or pamphlet, which contains material harmful to minors anywhere minors are lawfully admitted."[26] Each day a person is in violation of this section is considered a separate Class C misdemeanor.

The burden of proving that the material is displayed is on the state, and for purposes of this statute, material is not considered "displayed" if it is:

- placed in "binder racks" that cover the lower two thirds of the material, so long as the viewable one third is not harmful to minors;

- located at least five and one half feet from the floor; and
- reasonable steps are taken to prevent minors from perusing the material; or
- it is sealed with the cover opaquely wrapped if cover material is harmful to minors; or
- it is placed out of sight underneath the counter; or
- it is out of view of minors and located in an area restricted to adults.

The statute does not apply in a situation where a minor is accompanied by his or her parent or guardian except that, even then, minors may not enter an area restricted to adults.[27] Similar "variable obscenity" laws restricting for minors material that falls short of being obscene and thus is permissible for adults have been upheld by federal courts[28] as a valid exercise of government's legitimate concern for the welfare of minors.

In addition to these statutes concerning obscene materials and adult pornography made available to minors, the "Tennessee Protection of Children Against Sexual Exploitation Act of 1990"[29] makes it unlawful to knowingly possess, promote, sell, distribute, transport, purchase or exchange material showing a minor engaged in sexual activity or patently offensive simulated sexual activity or to use or permit a minor to participate in the performance or production of such material.

Other Tennessee Laws Concerning Obscenity

In Tennessee, "obscene or patently offensive bumper stickers, window signs, or other markings on a motor vehicle which are visible to other drivers" are prohibited.[30] The stated purpose of this statute is to avoid distracting other drivers and thereby reduce accidents.

Films depicting sexual conduct, as defined in the obscenity statute, must be shown within a closed area away from the view of persons who do not wish to see them.[31] Further, a theater with more than one screen must supervise customers to prevent minors from purchasing a ticket to a movie rated "G" or "PG" attraction and then viewing a film designated "R" or "X."[32] When the criminal code was revised in 1989, a penalty was specified by this statute for the first time. A violation is a Class A misdemeanor.[33]

Prosecuting Obscenity

In Tennessee the obscenity statutes may be enforced by either criminal actions or by actions for injunctive relief, or both, and such actions may be commenced simultaneously and proceed independently of each other.[34] A criminal action requires a criminal indictment or a warrant issued by a judge of any court of record. Such action shall begin only with the prior knowledge and written approval of the district attorney general or any assistant district attorney general.[35]

Statutory provision is made for a speedy trial where a temporary restraining order or temporary or permanent injunction has been issued. In such a proceeding, the defendant has no right to a trial by jury.[36] If a final order or judgment of injunction is entered, the clerk of the court in the county in which the proceedings were brought is directed to hold the allegedly obscene material to be used as evidence in a criminal proceeding. However, if no indictment is returned within six months, the stature directs that the clerk shall destroy the material.[37]

The obscenity statute in force before the 1989 revision of the state criminal code authorized an injunction to restrain the future showing of films alleged to be obscene. This provision was declared in violation of the First, Fifth, and Fourteenth amendments to the federal constitution.[38] Other cases have held that the state has the burden of proving that material is obscene and thus without constitutional protection[39] and that witnesses giving affidavits are not required to have viewed a work in its entirety. A 1975 case held that defendants in an obscenity case could not refuse to produce in open court the material alleged on the grounds that to do so would be self-incriminating.[40]

The Tennessee Court of Criminal Appeals ruled in a 1977 case that it was prejudicial to have a jury read the allegedly obscene material out of court, in the jury room under the supervision of jury officers but excluding parties and counsel in the case.[41]

Endnotes

1. As recently as 1989, the Tennessee Court of Criminal Appeals held that the Constitution of Tennessee does not protect all speech and that the state has the power, within Article 1, §19, to regulate obscenity. State v. Rollins, 785 S.W.2d 129.

2. See, e.g., State v. Martin, 719 S.W.2d 522 (Tenn. 1986).

3. See, e.g., Chief Justice Berger's majority opinion in Miller v. California, 413 U.S. 15, 93 S.Ct. 2607 (1973).

4. T.C.A. 39-17-901 to 39-17-920.

5. See, e.g., Taylor v. State ex rel Kirkpatrick, 529 S.W.2d 692 (Tenn. 1975), cert denied, 429 U.S. 930, 97 S.Ct. 337 (1976); State v. Runions, 654 S.W.2d 407 (Tenn. Crim. App. 1983); State v. Davis 654 S.W.2d 688 (Tenn. Crim. App. 1983); State v. Hunt, 660 S.W.2d 513 (Tenn. Crim. App. 1983), cert denied 466 U.S. 944, 104 S.Ct. 1928 (1984); State v. Murphy, 678 S.W.2d 913 (Tenn. Crim. App. 1983); State v. Frazier, 683 S.W.2d 346 (Tenn. Crim. App. 1984); State v. Summers, 692 S.W.2d 439 (Tenn. Crim. App. 1985); State v. Martin, 719 S.W.2d 522 (Tenn. 1986); State v. Rollins, 785 S.W.2d 129 (Tenn. Crim. App. 1989).

6. In addition to being a Class A misdemeanor, the statute provides that any corporation or business entity that violates this section shall be fined from $10,000 to $50,000. A similar provision in the former Tennessee obscenity statutes was upheld against a challenge that it violated the equal protection and due process clauses. State v. Murphy, 678 S.W.2d 913 (Tenn. Crim. App. 1983).

7. T.C.A. 39-17-902.

8. Id.

9. Id.(e).

10. Miller v. California, 413 U.S. 15, 93 S. Ct. 2607, 37 L. Ed. 2d 419.

11. T. C. A. 39-17-901(10).

12. Mishkin v. New York, 383 U.S. 502 at 508-509, 86 S.Ct. 958 at 963-964 (1966).

13. State v. Pendergrass, 795 S.W.2d 150 (Tenn. Crim. App. 1989), appeal denied, cert. denied, 110 S.Ct. 3215 (1989).

14. T. C. A. 39-17-901(2). The definition of "community" as set forth in the former provisions was held constitutional. State v. Frazier, 683 S.W.2d 346 (Tenn. Crim. App. 1984).

15. State v. Murphy, 678 S.W.2d 913 (Tenn. Crim. App. 1983).

16. Id. (11).

17. Id. (12).

18. Id.(14).

19. T.C.A. 39-17-901(1).

20. State v. Pendergrass, 795 S.W.2d 150 (Tenn. Crim. App. 1989), appeal denied, cert. denied, 110 S.Ct. 3215 (1989).

21. T.C.A. 39-17-902(b).

22. Id.(d).

23. T.C.A. 39-17-911.

24. T.C.A. 39-17-901(6).

25. T.C.A. 39-17-901(4).

26. T.C.A. 39-17-914.

27. Id.(b)(6).

28. See, e.g., Ginsberg v. New York, 390 U.S. 629, 635 n. 88 (1968).

29. T.C.A. 39-17-1001 to 39-17-1005.

30. T.C.A. 55-8-187.

31. T.C.A. 39-17-907(a).

32. Id.(b).

33. Id.(c).

34. T.C.A. 39-17-908(b).

35. Id.(a).

36. T.C.A. 39-17-905(a)(b).

37. Id.(c).

38. News Mart, Inc. v. State ex rel. Webster, 561 S.W.2d 752 (Tenn. 1978).

39. New Rivieria Arts Theatre v. State ex rel. Davis, 219 Tenn. 652, 412 S.W.2d 890 (1967).

40. Taylor v. State ex rel Kirkpatrick, 529 S.W.2d 692 (Tenn. 1975), cert denied, 429 U.S. 930, 97 S.Ct. 337 (1976).

41. Brazelton v. State, 550 S.W.2d 7.

Tips for Avoiding Lawsuits

Writers, editors, publishers and advertising personnel face potential legal problems every day. Communications companies turn to attorneys to handle many types of legal matters like antitrust, labor disputes, contracts and postal regulations but journalists are expected to know enough general information about libel, privacy and copyright law to avoid lawsuits or to at least know when to seek expert legal advice.

Editors generally have four choices when reviewing a story for libel, privacy or copyright problems:

(a) Go with the story because it has no legal problems.

(b) Kill the story because it is libelous, invades privacy, infringes copyright or has other legal problems.

(c) Edit the story carefully to remove offending passages.

(d) Expect a lawsuit, but publish the story because it is important and is defensible if it provokes a lawsuit.

The decision to publish a dangerous-but-defensible-story must not be made lightly and should not be made by one person acting alone. Staff members should alert their supervisors when dealing with a story or advertisement that has the potential of embroiling the organization in a lawsuit. Ultimately, the material may then be reviewed by the whole chain of command at the organization, and attorneys may become part of the decision-making process.

Cost of a Lawsuit

While crusading publishers who emphasize social responsibility over balance sheets are valued in journalistic circles, the tremendous cost of a lawsuit—even one that a news organization can win—is an important factor in deciding whether to publish. Is the story worth the cost of a lawsuit? It might not be, especially for a small publication or a company with few financial reserves.

A lawsuit is an immense drain on time and energy that needs to be directed at the business of publishing. A small staff may be unable to meet deadlines if reporters and editors are spending time meeting with lawyers and sitting in a courtroom day after day during pretrial motions, jury selection, the trial itself and perhaps the appeals process.

In addition to time and energy, monetary costs can be staggering. A 1991 study put the average cost of defending a libel suit through a trial at $175,000.[1] That is for legal costs alone. The average damage award for libel now exceeds that of medical malpractice or product liability. In 1985, the average medical malpractice damage award was $650,000, and the average product liability award was $750,000, as compared with $2 million for libel. During 1990 and 1991, juries awarded winning plaintiffs in libel trials an average of about $9 million each, according to figures from the Libel Defense Resource Center.

Libel insurance isn't a complete solution either because costs of libel insurance premiums have more than tripled in recent years, and more increases are expected. Too, policies being written often provide less coverage than they did in earlier years. For example, insurance contracts today often exclude the costs of defending suits.

Dealing with Disgruntled Readers or Viewers

Listen to Complaints

Common courtesy and a caring attitude can sometimes head off expensive lawsuits. Disgruntled readers who call the newsroom with a complaint should never be passed from one person to another or treated with the "Hey,-we've-got-a-crazy-on-the-line" approach.

Assuming that the story is fair and balanced, the editor or publisher may be able to convince the would-be plaintiff that a lawsuit is a waste of time and money. Unfortunately, they may never get an opportunity to placate an angry person if newsroom personnel fail to exercise common courtesy when dealing with angry readers.

The majority of more than 700 libel plaintiffs who were interviewed as part of a research project[2] said that a lawyer was not the first person called after they became upset about something they read in a newspaper or magazine or heard broadcast. First the distraught person contacted the offending publisher or broadcaster either with a personal visit to the newsroom or a telephone call. The person was upset and concerned about perceived harm to their reputations and about emotional distress, rather than financial damage.

After that initial contact, however—after being treated rudely—most plaintiffs said they were no longer just upset and hurt. They were angry. Then came the call to a lawyer. What could have been a golden opportunity for the media to head off a lawsuit became a golden opportunity for an attorney, especially one who was hired on an hourly fee rather than contingency-fee basis.

The media can't be expected to satisfy all agitated complainers, even if the publisher or station manager were willing to yield to every demand. But media personnel can be expected to refrain from rudeness.

The following actions are recommended for newsroom managers:

- Insist that everyone in the newsroom understands the power of the press to hurt people and that everyone gives courtesy a high priority.
- Make one person responsible for dealing with complaints. Be sure that person has good human relations skills. If financially possible, select someone who is not responsible for news coverage because editors don't have time to bird-dog complaints. Too, the qualities and skills that make a person a good editor or news director are not necessarily the same qualities that make for good people skills.
- Develop policy and procedure for addressing complaints. Put those policies and procedures in writing and make sure that everyone in the newsroom knows what they are.
- Deal harshly with any employee who sits on a complaint and doesn't direct it to the designated person.

Correct Errors

Two trends during the past few years show that newspapers treat reader complaints seriously: more papers regularly publish corrections columns, and more newspapers have created the position of ombudsman or reader representative. In an earlier era, editors did not want to admit that they made mistakes, but now many papers publicly correct errors that are brought to editors' attention.

Readers can talk back to their newspapers through letters to the editor, of course, but most are not motivated to spend time and effort writing letters. More will take the time to phone the paper and report errors, and those who do seem to appreciate the opportunity to talk with someone specially designated as the "reader representative." Where questions of news judgment and standard journalistic practices are concerned, the reader representative often can satisfy angry readers simply by explaining journalistic practices.

Smaller newspapers rarely have someone on the payroll to serve solely as a reader representative, but small papers, like their larger counterparts, often publish a regular corrections column. Newspapers vary in their policies about what kinds of errors they acknowledge and the prominence they give to corrections columns. Some papers give corrections columns prominent treatment in the front section while others relegate the column to a less noticeable spot.

Along with the corrections, some papers tell readers how each error was made, such as "incorrect information supplied by a source," "a reporting error" or "a copy editing error." Some papers, in addition to correcting the error, go a step further by apologizing for making the error. Regardless of specific policies on the content of regularly published corrections columns, they serve as one more quality-control device for newspapers and can help enhance credibility with readers.

Publishing a correction is not necessarily the same thing as publishing a retraction, however. If a paper or broadcast station receives a demand for a retraction, it is a good idea to consult legal counsel concerning whether to publish a retraction and its specific wording. These can be important considerations if a libel suit results from the original story. While a retraction is not a complete defense for libel, but it might mitigate damages.

News-Gathering and Editing Precautions

Avoiding clearly libelous stories or ones that invade privacy or infringe on copyrights should begin at the reporting stage. Reporters must understand that they can defame someone at the news-gathering stage, even before a story is written.

Accuracy and Fairness

Accuracy, accuracy, accuracy. Journalists have heard about it from every journalism teacher, editor or news director they have encountered. Accuracy cannot be over emphasized.

Attention to accuracy must start at the very beginning of the news-gathering process when the idea for a story is conceived. Reporters should avoid approaching a story with preconceived notions that the subject of the story was a good guy or a bad guy; that corruption existed in the police department; that the school superintendent was incompetent. Journalists who approached a story with a preconceived idea about how it is supposed to turn out tend to look for evidence to support that viewpoint and give short shrift to contradictory information.

Editors and news directors should question reporters about whether they examined all angles of a story and relied upon the most credible sources.

To head off lawsuits, the editors must check stories for fairness and balance, ensuring that the reporter has supported generalizations with evidence from interviews and record searches. Editors should ascertain that reporters have contacted people who might be damaged by the story. Denials, if made, should be included in the story.

Remember that truth is a defense for libel, but it is not a defense for most privacy cases. For example, private information that is highly offensive to a reasonable person is actionable as an invasion of privacy, even though the information is true.

Too, truth is often difficult to prove in a libel suit. While the plaintiff has the burden of proving the falsity of a story, the news organization will try to counter with arguments to support the accuracy of the story because the burden of proof is a distinction that is often difficult for juries to make.

Literal accuracy is not always enough to defend against a libel suit, because literal accuracy is not necessarily the same as truth. One Tennessee newspaper was sued for libel after publishing that a woman shot her husband when she found him in the company of another woman. That was literally accurate, but the story falsely implied adultery. The truth was that the woman entered a residence where her husband was sitting in the living room in the company of several other people, including the "other woman's" husband.

A story that accurately reports that someone made a false and defamatory statement about someone else may be grounds for a successful libel suit. Unless the charge is made during a privileged situation, like a city council meeting, it is not safe to republish defamatory statements. For example, to publish that someone said that a local merchant was dishonest would be dangerous unless the newspaper has independent proof of a pattern of dishonesty or unless the publication is made in one of the few jurisdictions that recognizes neutral reportage as a libel defense.

Tennessee law does not recognize neutral reportage as a defense. The general rule in Tennessee, as in most states, is that one who republishes a defamatory quotation is just as guilty of libel as the original defamer.

In the several jurisdictions where neutral reportage has been recognized, these conditions apply:

- the accusation must be made by a responsible person or organization;
- must be about a public figure or public official;
- must concern a public issue;
- must be reported fairly and accurately;
- the story must be balanced by giving the accused's point of view

Double check routine facts and stories because those are often the basis for a lawsuit. Research has shown that more than half the libel suits against newspapers during the 1970s and 1980s were based on stories that appeared on inside pages. About 45 percent of the suits were for front-page stories.[3]

The following words and expressions should raise red flags during the editing process:

has AIDS
adultery
atheist
adulteration of products
altered records
attempted suicide

bad moral character
bankrupt
bigamist
blackmail
bribery
brothel
buys votes
cheats
collusion
criminal
kept woman
Ku Klux Klan
liar
mental disease
Nazi
peeping Tom
perjurer
corruption
coward
crook
deadbeat
double-crosser
drug addict
ex-convict
scoundrel
shyster
sneak
sold influence
fool
fraud
illegal gambling
graft
hypocrite
illegitimate
illicit relations
incompetent
infidelity
Jekyll-Hyde personality
sold out
spy
stuffed the ballot box
suicide
swindle
unethical
unprofessional
villain

Interviewing

Third-party publication is sufficient to establish slander, so reporters are treading on dangerous ground if they use the ploy of pretending to know more than they do in order to gain information. A reporter fishing for information, should not tell a source, "We already know that Jones a dishonest cop. We just want your comments." Instead, try something such as, "We're looking into Jones' conduct as a police officer, and we'd like to get your comments."

Journalists should use the same courtesy when gathering information as in dealing with angry readers, listener or viewers. Being aggressive in pursuit of a story does not necessarily equate with being rude or insensitive. Reporters can get graphic stories while maintaining courtesy and dignity.

Ambush journalism isn't the norm in news gathering. Reporters don't have to push a microphone and lights into the face of a grieving mother and ask "How does it feel to have your child run over by a truck?"

In the interest of accuracy, fairness and balance, subjects of accusations or unflattering comments should be contacted for their response. If the subject denies the accusations, include the denial in the published story. This may help establish lack of actual malice if a libel suit or false light privacy suit results from the story.

Credible Sources

Precedent teaches that courts will consider the credibility of sources as a factor in determining whether a story was published with actual malice. Reporters should always interview the most credible sources available and more than one such source, if possible. Except for the most routine stories, avoid single-source stories.

Consider the motivations of sources. Do they have a "hidden agenda," a history of bad feeling toward the subject of the story, or some other reason to present biased information?

Don't become a slave to "official" sources especially government sources. While beat reporters will have regular sources, they shouldn't become complacent about cultivating new sources on the beat.

Reluctant Sources

If a person who might be damaged by a story is reluctant to talk to a reporter and is avoiding phone calls, editors and news directors should not publish the story with a simple, "Jones was unavailable for comment."

Make sure that the reporter goes to extra lengths to talk with the person. Have the reporter make several calls to Jones' business, home, lawyer, family, usual hangouts. In talking to people at all these places, the reporter also may gain important information for a better story. Leave messages for the reluctant source.

Establish a record of attempts to get him to talk. These extra efforts may be important if the publication is sued for libel because repeated attempts to reach the source and information from sources close to him may help show a lack of fault on the part of the press.

Confidential Sources

Some news organizations have a policy of never allowing anonymous sources to be used except in exceptional circumstances, arguing that the public is better served if the source is known. Also, the story is stronger, and news organization has a better legal case if the story becomes the basis for a lawsuit.

If a story based on a confidential source becomes the subject of a libel suit, the defendant reporter and news organization may be unable to argue that the story was published without actual malice because juries consider source credibility in determining actual malice. If the jury does not know the identity of the source, credibility cannot be judged.

The Tennessee shield law does not apply when a defendant in a libel suit tries to defend allegedly defamatory information that came from confidential sources. In such instances, reporters are faced with the dilemma of violating confidentiality or having the judge instruct the jury to assume that no source existed for the information in question.

If faced with a story of Watergate magnitude, reporters may want to meet "Deep Throat" in the parking garage in the dark of night. But too often the use of anonymous sources seems to readers to be just an excuse for "weasel" journalism and its attendant sloppy, lazy reporting. The use of anonymous sources can be an invitation to exaggerate, embellish, slant or take a cheap shot.

Information supplied by an anonymous source should be verified independently by at least one other source, preferably by more than one. If an anonymous source is used, explain to readers why the identity is being withheld. Give readers enough information to establish the source's credibility, which, of course, is sometimes difficult to do without revealing the identity.

If conditions were imposed on an interview, and if the reporter agreed to those conditions, editors should consider carefully the ramifications of violating such agreements. Courts may consider such oral promises to be binding contracts and thus subject to damage awards if broken.[4]

Trespassing

Being in hot pursuit of a story does not excuse trespassing. Reporters and camera crews have no legal right to enter private property without consent, even if the purpose of the story is to expose wrongdoing on the part of the property owner, and even if journalists are working in cooperation with law enforcement officials.[5]

Journalists have no legal right to accompany protesters onto private property a nuclear power plant, for example to get a story. The power plant operators may legally restrict reporters and cameras to a particular "viewing" area, even though the view from that area might not result in pictures as good as those the photographer could get from the vantage point of the protesters.[6]

Likewise, in some jurisdictions it is considered trespassing for a reporter or photographer to accompany public officials onto private property. Court decisions are mixed on this question.[7]

To be safe, news personnel should have permission from the property owner preferably in writing or with witnesses to oral consent. If the property owner is present, observes the reporter or photographer and doesn't object, then "implied consent" might be argued. But journalists have little recourse if the owner asks them to leave the property.

A general rule is that anything that can be seen from a public place is not private, so it is permissible for a photographer to stand in a public area to take pictures of something happening on private property. Yet, it would be hard to defend a photographer who climbed a seldom-scaled cliff or a ladder to take pictures with a telephoto lens of activities behind a fenced yard.

Another form of trespass or intrusion is surreptitious taping. Most states allow one-party consent; that is, the reporter may record an interview or telephone conversation without telling the source, but a dozen or so states require both parties to give consent for taping. Most states, including Tennessee, allow one-party consent, meaning that journalists can legally record interviews or telephone conversations without telling sources.

Many journalists and news organizations, however, question the ethics of such news-gathering procedure. Even where it is legal, reporter and photographers should talk with their supervisors about organizational policy before using hidden recorders or cameras.

Check the Clip File

Don't forget to check the clip file or data bank at your own news organization. This is often a quick, easy way to verify information. This assumes, of course, that the clip file is accurate. Establish some sort of procedure whereby a note accompanies clips if inaccuracies are discovered so that they are not repeated in subsequent stories.

Reporters' or editors' failure to check in-house files could be used against a news organization as evidence of negligence in a libel suit. During discovery, a plaintiff's attorney could learn that information contained in those files could have headed off an erroneous, defamatory story.

Stories About Lawsuits

Journalists should be especially alert to libel and privacy dangers when handling stories about civil lawsuits or criminal cases. Never publish a story saying that someone "may" or "plans to" file a civil suit. Be sure that the suit has been filed and, depending on the laws of the state, that some action has been taken on the suit. Make sure that the complaint is accurately quoted or paraphrased once the suit is filed.

In criminal cases, double check all key facts—the name of the accused, address, specific charge. Use the suspect's middle name or initial to avoid confusion with someone who has a similar name. Manslaughter and murder are not the same charge, so be exact.

Let the court, not your news organization, judge the guilt or innocence of the defendant. The word "alleged," as in, "alleged axe murderer John Jones" does not necessarily protect from a libel suit. Grammatically, the description "alleged axe murderer" can be understood to mean that Jones is an axe murderer who also happens to be accused, which is hardly what the writer meant, unless the writer does not accept the innocent-until-proven-guilty principle of American jurisprudence.

Don't publish defamatory out-of-court statements. For example, don't quote the police chief's remark that "We've got an air-tight case against this killer John Jones" unless the chief says it in a privileged situation.

When reporting what was said during an open court or other privileged situation, be sure to get it right and to present a fair account of what happened during the privileged proceeding. Inaccuracy can defeat the privilege.

Be sure that quotations from court testimony accurately reflect the context of the testimony. A libel suit resulted, for example, from a newspaper story about a trial in which a man was accused of cruelty to animals. After describing in some detail the customary procedures used in breeding pigs, the defendant said something to the effect, "If that is cruelty to animals, then I am guilty." The last part of that sentence, taken out of context, created the damaging, erroneous impression that the defendant had pled guilty to the charge.

In the interest of fairness, the outcome of both civil and criminal cases, especially if the criminal defendant is acquitted, should be published in a position of prominence similar to the story about the defendant's arrest or indictment.

Headlines, Promos, Quote Boxes

Headlines, broadcast promos and news breaks, and quote boxes all are potentially defamatory. Use attribution in headlines or broadcast promos that state opinions.

Promos and quote boxes particularly are problematic because quotations taken out of context may be damaging. Generally, courts consider stories as a whole, along with headlines and quote boxes, when judging defamation or invasion of privacy, but some courts have reasoned that many readers may not go beyond the headline, which can leave erroneous and damaging impressions. The same applies for broadcast promos and news breaks designed to lead viewers into newscasts.

Newsroom Talk

Journalists are reminded to be careful about what they say in the newsroom or write in a memo. The Alton Telegraph case[8] taught us that even unpublished memos can be dangerous.

Don't sit around the newsroom making wild exaggerations about investigative pieces or other sensitive stories. Such statements could come back to haunt a news organization during a libel trial as a plaintiff's attorney works to convince a jury that the "state of mind"[9] of reporters or editors during story preparation was conducive to "reckless disregard for truth."

Scoop Mentality

Being first with the news is still important to the ratings or circulation figures, but the "scoop mentality" can cause trouble. The world won't end and your competition, if you have any, won't either if you spend another day working on a story. It's better to be safe than first with the story.

Photos and Film Footage

Editors and news directors who use file pictures out of context risk portraying photo subjects in a false light. For example, a picture of a child hurt in an accident was appropriately used in a newsworthy context in a newspaper. However, the same picture was actionable as false light privacy when used by a national magazine to illustrate a story headlined "They ask to be killed," which discussed the harm that people often cause through carelessness.[10]

Photo Captions and Voice Overs

A photograph or film footage may be safe from a lawsuit, but the accompanying caption or voiceover can be dangerous if it defames or depicts someone in a false light. For example, a broadcast station opens itself to a libel or false light privacy suit by showing footage of young women sitting on the front steps of a high school, with the name of the school clearly visible in the background, while an announcer talks about a court decision concerning abortion rights of teenagers.

Inaccurate and incomplete identifications in captions have also been the basis for lawsuits.

Opinion

The common law libel defense of fair comment and criticism provides some protection for opinion, but journalists must use precautions to clearly distinguish fact from opinion and to ensure accuracy of factual statements.

Although letters to the editor are clearly the opinions of letter writers, the information used to support those opinions is not protected if it is false and defamatory. If is also important to verify the identity of letter writers before publishing.

Just as in editorials, specific facts should be given to support opinions in critical reviews. Say, for example, that the steak was tough and the salad greens were wilted at a particular restaurant, rather than simply that the food was awful and not worth buying. Never imply that the food will make customers sick, as in "Don't eat at Joe's unless you are in the mood to have your stomach pumped."

Avoid repeating old restaurant reviews. You had tough steak and wilted lettuce at Joe's a year ago. Don't use that old review. Give Joe another chance and then write a new review. Maybe Joe got a new cook or a new beef supplier.

For editorial cartoons, sometimes wild exaggeration is the best policy so that no reasonable person could confuse fact with opinion. A study of libel suits filed between 1970 and 1987 revealed that 22 involved editorial cartoons, and the media won all except two of those.

Ed Williams, editorial page editor for the *Charlotte*, N.C., *Observer*, gives these instructions to editorial-page writers and editors at his newspaper:

- Get the facts straight.
- Be sure facts are facts and opinions are opinions.
- Read it on the page proofs.
- Talk with the paper's lawyers before publication if the subject matter is touchy.

Advertising

Broadcast and print media should not use names, pictures or any likeness of a person for advertising without getting written consent. Be sure that the person is legally empowered to enter into a contract. For minors, you need to get consent signed by parents or legal guardians. In addition, make sure that the consent covers the expected use of the name or likeness.

It is permissible to use previously published articles, photographs or film footage as a sample of the content of the newscast, paper or magazine in a promotional piece, for example so long as there is no implication the people shown are endorsing your station or publication.[11]

The fact that a defamatory statement appeared in an advertisement does not excuse the owner of the publication or broadcast station. It isn't sufficient to argue that you simply published what the ad agency sent. You are responsible for what appears in your publication.

On the other hand, owners generally are not held legally responsible for false claims made in advertisements, although the consumer's perception of a publication's credibility may be tied to the type of advertisements it publishes.

Copyright

A key principle of copyright law is that facts and ideas cannot be copyrighted. No person or news organization can "own" the facts concerning a newsworthy story or the idea of covering a particular subject. But the manner of expression—the specific patterns of words and the pictures used to tell the story or discuss the idea—can be protected from infringement by others. Plagiarism is both illegal and unethical.

Many publications may use the same article through contractual agreements with news services and other suppliers of syndicated material. Members of the Associated Press, for example, agree to share spontaneous local news stories with other AP members, who have the right to use such "spot news" stories verbatim. However, stories resulting from individual enterprise and initiative that are copyrighted by the originating news organization cannot be used by fellow AP members without permission.

The fair use defense allows publications to use brief quotations from a copyrighted work for critical reviews or scholarly work. Key ideas behind the fair use doctrine are that the one who copies must add substantial independent work and that such copying should be in the public interest.

While no formula exists concerning how much copying is permissible under the fair use doctrine, journalists should exercise special care when using verbatim or closely paraphrased passages from copyrighted material. Several paragraphs may be acceptable in some circumstances, whereas a single line from a poem or song may be grounds for a successful infringement suit. Much depends on the amount and nature of the material that the copier adds to the original work.

These are factors that courts consider when deciding whether copyrighted material has been used fairly:

- The purpose and character of the use, including whether such use is of a commercial nature or is for nonprofit educational purposes.
- The nature of the copyrighted work.
- The amount and substantiality of the portion used in relation to the copyrighted work as a whole.
- The effect of the use upon the potential market for or value of the copyrighted work.

Current copyright law provides that a work is protected as soon as it is "fixed in tangible form." It no longer has to be published in order to be copyrighted. Thus, journalists should avoid using any printed material, film, music or material fixed in any other tangible medium without written consent unless the use can qualify for the fair use defense.

Unpublished letters are eligible for copyright protection, courts have ruled. Journalists should be aware that the author of a letter, not the recipient, is the copyright owner and thus controls use of the letter.

Know Your Rights and Responsibilities

Continuing Education

Dedicate some time to in-house training sessions. Even the old timers need to be reminded or brought up to date on changes in the law. New staff members, especially those who didn't attend journalism school, might never have learned anything about press law. Even journalism school graduates who had a course in communications law may not remember what they learned, and sometimes they need to be reminded that what they hear in the classroom does apply in the "real world."

You could probably get a journalism professor from a nearby college or perhaps an attorney to come to your station or newspaper for a training session. Just be sure to invite a professor or attorney who is especially knowledgeable about communications law. It is a specialized field, and not all journalism professors or attorneys know or can be expected to know its intricacies.

Keep trade publications, like *Publishers Auxiliary, Broadcasting, Presstime,* and *Editor & Publisher,* readily available in the newsroom and have staffers read them for advice on avoiding lawsuits. It can also be helpful to have some current media law books on hand and encourage the staff to read them.

Seek Competent Legal Advice

Advice about many communications law problems is just a phone call away from the Tennessee Press Association or from the Reporters Committee for Freedom of the Press or the FOI Center in Washington, D.C.

The toll-free telephone number for the TPA Media Hotline is **1-800-531-5041**. Non-daily newspapers can subscribe to this service for an annual fee of 1 cent per subscriber ($100 minimum). The subscription fee for daily newspapers is 2 cents per subscriber ($200 minimum). The service is also available on an "as-needed" basis for $75 per call.

The Reporters Committee telephone number for legal assistance is **1-800-FFOI-AID.**

A preventive approach is often better and a lot less expensive than a defensive approach. When reviewing sensitive stories, it may be worth time and money to seek an attorney's advice to head off suits rather than respond to them after they are filed. The state of Tennessee does not certify specialists in the law, but look for an attorney who has experience in communications law.

Encourage your attorney to help you figure out how to get the story safely on the air or into print, rather than spiking it. In addition to reviewing sensitive stories, an attorney can help win access to records and meetings that you might have trouble with.

Editors, publishers, news directors, or station managers, however, should be the final arbiter. Don't let attorneys usurp the editorial role.

Endnotes

1. John Soloski and Randall Bezanson, "Libel Law and Journalistic Malpractice: A Preliminary Analysis of Fault in Libel Litigation," paper presented at the Association for Education in Journalism and Mass Communication annual convention, August 1991.

2. Randall P. Bezanson, Gilbert Cranberg, and John Soloski, Libel Law and the Press: Myth and Reality (New York: The Free Press, 1987).

3. Id.

4. See Cohen v. Cowles Media Co., 111 S. Ct. 2513 (1991).

5. See, for example, Dietemann v. Time, Inc. 449 F.2d 245 (9th Cir. 1971).

6. Oklahoma v. Bernstein, 5 Media Law Rptr. 2313 (Okla. D.C., Rogers County 1980).

7. Florida Pub. Co. v. Fletcher, 340 So.2d 914 (Fla. 1976); Anderson v. WROC-TV, 109 Misc.2d 904, 7 Media Law Rptr. 1987 (1981).

8. See chapter on libel.

9. See Herbert v Lando, 441 U.S. 153 (1979)

10. Leverton v. Curtis Pub. Co., 192 F.2d 974 (3d Cir. 1951).

11. See Booth v. Curtis Pub. Co., 223 N.Y.S.2d 737 (1962) and Namath v. Sports Illustrated, 39 N.Y.2d 897 (1976).